Speak the Truth: Justice for Miss America
The True Story of Kristine Bunch vs. State of Indiana.

First Printing, 2017

ISBN-13: 978-1546546580

ISBN-10: 1546546588

Edited by: Ruth Fuller

Cover Photo: Andy Goodwin

DEDICATION

For the Innocent: may you find your justice.

Contents

DEDICATION...3

Foreword 6

Prologue: A Unique Friendship 11

Chapter One: Small town 29

Chapter Two: Tony's life 39

Chapter Three: Charged with Murder 42

Chapter Four: Five days in Hell 57

Chapter Five: Welcome to Indiana Women's Prison (IWP) 72

Chapter Six: A Promise with Empty Arms 82

Chapter Seven: Becoming Miss America 102

Chapter Eight: Murder Upheld 114

Chapter Nine: Bringing Awareness to her Darkness............................134

Chapter Ten: No Escape Plan for the Innocent....................144

Chapter Eleven: Building a Dream Team 151

Chapter Twelve: The Final Fight begins 167

Chapter Thirteen: A Deal Exchange for Innocence 177

Chapter Fourteen: Argument for Justice 194

Chapter Fifteen: 48 hours...................................200

Chapter Sixteen: The Reality of Freedom 204

Chapter Seventeen: Starting Over Again 229

Epilogue: Hard Road Home....................................247

Author's Note: 260

In Memoriam of Jane Ellen Raley 265

Acknowledgements: 267

Special Thanks from Kristine Bunch......................269

How You Can Help 273

ABOUT THE AUTHOR 275

Foreword

Miss America is a helluva title to be given. I received that title from a 15-year-old girl that I met in prison. I did not receive that title because I am a 6-foot-tall, size zero blonde. I received that title because I fought a battle inside myself every day to lock away the pain, stand tall and put a smile on my face. I know that people do this same thing every day, but not many are doing it inside of a maximum-security prison with a 60-year sentence hanging over their heads.

Meeting Donna inside that facility was a blessing. I had lost my son and I was pregnant with a second child that I knew I would have to give up. I was broken with wounds to my soul that will never be healed completely. Donna helped ease the pain. I needed a child to love and care for. Here was this sweet girl, thrown into an adult facility and she was struggling. I could give her all the hope and support she needed to survive

I taught Donna to stand tall and put a smile on her face. People will always try to bring you down but you never let them see it. This motto truly applies in prison where misery is dished out by many even the staff. It is not fit for human beings and it certainly was not fit for a young girl. My heart broke for her and I wanted to see her rise above. My plight seemed hopeless but hers was something that could be overcome.

I did not know that Donna would become a warrior for me. My dreams for her were to live life freely and find all the good that is in this world. I wanted her to walk away from the prison and never look back. Instead, she walked away from the prison but continued to hold onto me. Letters, phone calls, and visits continued after her release. She was my family...not by blood but through love, respect, and loyalty. Our hearts made us sisters.

When Donna and I spoke of this book, she said, "I want the world to see you as I do Miss America." Those words scared me. I did not want anyone to see my pain, my weaknesses or my issues. I believe that people can take those things and use them against you. I pulled my shoulders back, smiled and told her that I would be honored to have her share my story. While some may use my vulnerabilities against me, others will draw strength from it. I want my pain to have meaning and bring strength to others.

I expected a regular book. Instead, I read an emotional journey. I relived all the triumph and pain through Donna's words. I was stunned. I did not believe that she knew what was deep in my heart. I never realized how much she saw behind my smile or my encouraging words. Truly she was the only person able to share what is inside of me because she lived it with me and she continues

to live it.

I am amazed every time I look at Donna. She is a wonderful mother, devoted wife, and caring citizen. She looks for the good in the world and she believes that she can change things for the better. I say these words with great pride. I believe that I taught her those lessons. I know that I taught her self-worth and determination. Inside of a facility, I was able to give her all that I wanted to instill in my own child.

The story is not over instead it is evolving. I know what Miss America is supposed to do and I want to bring about change for others. I want to believe that we can all make a difference. I want to believe in the good. I want to continue to bring hope and teach lessons just like I did for my little sister, Donna. My pain is still invisible to so many but it drives me to fight for the things that I love and value. It reminds me that I am still alive and I have a duty to find the good in the world...to bring good to the world.

Donna's words have let me know that someone truly sees me. Not the façade that I put on, but me. The good, the bad and all that I hide. It is liberating to know that even though I have my head held high and a smile on my face, someone knows who I really am. Not the person they have seen in interviews or have read about, but me. Someone that loves and believes in me despite everything.

She is the reason that I continue to push forward and I strive to be Miss America. I pray that I make her as proud of me as I am of her.

-Kristine Bunch

Prologue: A Unique Friendship

I have always been the "baby." For the past twenty years, Kristine has called me her baby. The amount of love that is placed in that one simple word has molded my thinking on how all of my relationships should be and it has changed the way that I view all of my relationships over the years. She has made me into a woman that could be a good mother, sister, wife and friend to others. The relationship that we share is heaven sent.

Ironically, our journey into the adult judicial system began on the same day: July 5, 1995, as I was waived into the adult court and she was arrested. It would take 9 months for our paths to cross and for a relationship to form that would change both of our lives forever. We were destined to meet, even if it was in the worst place possible.

I arrived at Indiana Women's Prison on December 18, 1995, at the age of 14, making me the youngest child to be sent to a maximum-security prison in Indiana. It was one week before Christmas as the sheriff's car entered the back of the prison. through a series of chained fences and barb wires. I wondered if I would survive my 25-year sentence. My head felt weak as I walked into the prison, my hands and feet shackled. I was no longer a child. I had just become an adult.

Prison officials were unsure what to do with me as they scrambled to process me into the Department of Corrections (DOC) system. My first few hours were spent in a long hallway with several doors. One doorway was a bathroom where I had to stand naked for 10 minutes waiting to hear that I could take a cold shower to rinse the lice shampoo off my body and hair. Another door led to a room where I was asked a series of questions that would help the prison officials determine my state of mind. As the officer asked the questions, I cried. No, I am not going to make a bomb. No, I'm not going to get in a fight if someone talks about my crime. Never in my wildest dreams did I imagine that I would see and meet people who had answered yes to either of these questions.

Every inmate is sent to a unit to go through the rest of the intake process and wait for their classifications, which included future housing and job. I was put in a cell with a 24-year-old, the youngest woman that they had in intake. She was nice enough, but her stories were different than I had ever heard. She told stories of drug-fueled rages where she claimed she "lost control." She told stories of being so high that sleeping with random men for money was "normal." In less than 24 hours of being a D.O.C. inmate, I learned what some people would do for a fix.

I would soon see why my fears of dying inside this prison could happen. New Year's Eve, after the lights went out, I laid on my bed looking out at the grounds of I.W.P., the yard brightly lit up, and I saw four or five officers running toward a building that I couldn't see. When I told my cellmate, she got excited and we continued to watch together. Minutes later, officers carried a bloody woman to the infirmary followed by another woman who was walking, but was also bloody. I could hear the yelling of the walking inmate claiming that she was attacked and I watched as the officers struggled to contain her. In excitement, my cellmate tossed out theories about the fight. I closed my eyes and quietly cried, wondering if I would be the next victim.

The next day, I welcomed a change. Intake was boring, and all the stories of violence scared me. I knew most women were just trying to scare me, and it worked. I was classified to a dorm with allot of women with mental illnesses. There were mandatory groups that were led by the dorm counselors that were meant to specialize in grief, child abuse, or anger. The meetings were mandatory for all dorm members and were meant to be therapy for the inmates. I was told that I would be safer there. My "bunkie" was a 21-year old woman who claimed that she killed her boyfriend's four-year old because she was suffering from a mental breakdown brought on by the child's crying.

I soon met Mariah*[1], another young offender at a group outside of my normal groups within the dorm. This group was

[1] (name changed to protect identity)

designed to give the offenders that were young, an outlet among other younger offenders. It was a safe place to express their fears and emotions that older offenders might not understand nor care about. It was this group that helped me survive those early days. In the group, I was surrounded by other inmates who were 25 years old or younger. It was here that I met Mariah.

Mariah had been at the prison since she was 16, and she was still alive. That gave me hope that I could survive too. As I waited on the D.O.C. commissar decision on whether I would stay at the prison or go to a juvenile treatment center, Mariah helped me adjust to my day-to-day life. She became my ally as I struggled to handle prison life, especially living in my dorm. In the dorm, I had to attend groups that specialized in grief and child abuse. However, it was not a group that was intended to help child abuse survivors. I was forced to listen to these women talk in detail about their crimes. I remember one woman recalled how she killed her child by warming a metal spoon on the stove and slowing killing her child. She recalled how she must have burnt the baby 70 times or more. The baby couldn't take the pain of the

burns and died due to the burns suffered. As she told the story,

she held a baby doll and stroked the doll's hair. It was creepy.

None of this helped me when I spoke about my own child abuse.

They said I couldn't understand their pain because I never had

been a mother, as if that somehow justified their abusive acts,

because it was all due to the pressures of being a mother.

After the D.O.C. made the decision that I would remain at

the prison instead of going to the treatment center, the ACLU filed

a lawsuit against the State of Indiana on my behalf. This lawsuit

made my life even harder inside the walls. I was surrounded by

the people I was suing. There were many times that I questioned

the lawsuit due to the comments that I was hearing from my

dorm counselors and director of the dorm. Even some officers

made comments that I was overreacting to my prison term. I felt I

had no one to rely on, which is why my relationship with Mariah

was crucial to my survival. She also had a new friend- a friend who

also needed her.

I first met Kristine Bunch at a picnic that the prison offered every two weeks during the summer months. She was pregnant and Mariah doted on her, making me jealous. As Kristine's son did cartwheels in her stomach, Mariah focused solely on the baby and not me. As exciting as it was to watch Kristine's stomach move, I was envious of the attention. The summer went by and the lawsuit was given a court date.

Sitting at a card table in the gym, I waited for Kristine to arrive. I was nervous because my interaction with her had been limited to time spent with Mariah. Mariah was starting her college classes and she still wanted me to get out of the dorm, so she set up this meeting with Kristine. I didn't know what to expect from Kristine.

I watched other prisoners come in and worried that Kristine wouldn't like me without Mariah. I was now fifteen, and struggling inside the prison. I had recently gone to court begging for a transfer to a juvenile treatment center. I had issues being the youngest prisoner. That is one of the reasons that I loved my time with Mariah—she understood what it felt to be locked up inside prison as a minor. She never treated me like a child and, strangely, never treated me like an adult.

When Kristine finally approached my table, she had two pops and nutty bars—my favorite. I remember thinking that she already knew me, but being the brat, I was, I didn't acknowledge it. Maybe to break the ice, Kristine said something that I will never forget. She said, "I know that I am not your first choice, but I am happy to be here." I remember looking at her and thinking, why? I was not a special person, nor was I a good person. Yet she was glad to be sitting here with me and wanted me to know this.

For the next two hours, we talked, laughed, and shed a few tears. We talked about the charges for which we were imprisoned. I was guarded about my crime—I felt that no one would understand the truth—but Kristine was adamant that she was innocent. I believed her, even though I didn't understand how someone that was innocent could be in prison.

After that first evening, Kristine and I hung out almost every day. I could tell her all about my drama—there was always something—and she listened and advised me on how to handle the situations. She listened and never made me feel judged. We went to movies together and she always brought the snacks. I had something that I needed: a sister.

Kristine never treated me as her child, nor did she act like my best friend. She was a big sister who was there to listen to me complain about how unfair the system was, or to be there when the weight of my situation was too much to bear. There was never a time that I didn't know that she loved me. I may not have understood how she could love me, and there would be many tests that I would put her through. She stood her ground and I slowly realized that she was unbreakable against my ploys. She never judged me for the crime that I pled guilty to, and listened to me as I struggled to make sense of my new reality. The amount of patience that she had with me was incredible.

I knew that I wanted Kristine in my life forever. She

listened to me and didn't try to tell me to stop being a drama queen. She was there when I was trying to figure out my place in an adult world, although I was just a child. She went to extremes to see that I enjoyed the small things inside the prison walls. There was never a holiday or birthday that she didn't make me feel extra special.

When I turned sixteen, she carefully wrapped sixteen Tootsie Roll Pops into a beautiful bouquet. She spoiled me, even though we were living in a prison.

Even when we separated—when I was finally allowed to go a juvenile treatment facility from age sixteen until eighteen— we maintained contact. Everyone knew that I needed Krissy; she had become my biggest supporter. She called me every two weeks and wrote countless letters that were always filled with love. She even made me 21 hearts from pink paper that she carefully cut into the shape of hearts to hang in my bedroom windows so my room would be filled with heart sunshine. There were mornings that I woke to perfectly shaped shadows of hearts and I felt her love.

Although I was happy to be surrounded by my peers, I missed her. She was the one person that knew how to handle me during my hard times. I was her baby and she never let anyone forget that.

I returned to the prison at the age of eighteen, after getting my high school diploma. I came back on the day that college classes started. I spent the day getting reacquainted with the prison, and by the time my first college class started, I was exhausted. When I arrived at the education building for class, Kristine was waiting. Ignoring the prison's rule of no contact, we hugged and cried. I knew, in that moment, that I could finish my sentence with her support.

Having been gone for two years didn't do much to take the prison out of me. I struggled through my first semester of college. In fact, I was placed on academic probation and, thinking I was grown now, I tried to hide this from Kristine. Yet true to form, she found out. Being the way she is, she let me believe that I was in the clear.

One night I got a kite (a prison letter that we passed illegally to each other) telling me to go to REC and that she had a surprise for me. I was beyond excited, just knowing that she had made me Spam burgers—my favorite and my usual surprise from Kristine. When seven p.m. came and I dashed to the recreational building to set up our table and wait for her. Imagine my surprise to see her waiting... with my college books, which she had gotten from my other classmates. She chewed me out for about 30 minutes and reminded me that my college degree would allow me to get my sentence reduced, making my release date soon after I graduated. She listened to my excuses, that I was having trouble with my job and didn't have time to sleep anymore. I gave her every excuse I could, but she stood her ground. She gave me a choice: take college seriously, or find someone else to hang out with because she was too focused to be held back by quitters. With her help, I shaped up and even graduated a year early. I would have never gotten through adjusting back to prison and finishing my Bachelor's degree without her.

Even after my release in 2002, she remained my lifeline. I waited for letters and phone calls. My new surroundings were unfamiliar and I was scared, but still she was my biggest cheerleader. She told me I could do anything that I put my mind to. I struggled to find my way. I married a man, and from that marriage, I gained my two daughters, though the marriage failed. When I wrote Kristine to tell her that I was getting a divorce, I expected a different response than I got. "Good, he didn't deserve you" is what she said. It was that letter that made me realize my true value.

I didn't really understand Kristine's wrongful conviction until after my own release. I always believed in her innocence. She told me that she didn't do it, and that was all I needed to hear.

When I left the prison in 2002, at the age of 21, I was still a naïve child. Even as she was fighting for her freedom, she continued to guide me through my new challenges.

I spent hours researching her case and how the science of fires had changed since her conviction. I finally understood that she was wrongly convicted and for the first time, I understood how strong she really was. I would tell everyone that I had a big sister who was in prison and was innocent. I even tried to bring awareness to her case using the Facebook page "Bring Krissy Home." I needed her out.

Kristine's release came almost ten years after mine. I remember reading that she had been released and cried. I finally felt freed. We wasted no time reconnecting. I spoke to her on the phone the night of her release. I then hung up on her just so I could call her back. After years of her calling me, I wanted to call her- it was more real to me, and I could call her whenever I needed her, not having to wait until she called. As I went to sleep that night, I thanked God over and over for her being home. I knew that her journey wasn't over, but at least she was a phone call away. I made plans to see her that weekend.

Arriving there, I could barely wait for my new husband to park the truck before jumping out to run into Kristine's arms.

There was no search or barb wires that night, only air between us. That visit would be the first of many. We talk as much as we want and our calls can last for hours. She is always my first call when life's challenges are too much. I have my big sister with me.

Since her release in 2012, I have watched as Kristine struggles to live outside the prison walls. I saw how she learned to work a smart phone or manage a Facebook page. She was behind in technology, but she never gives up. I have also witnessed her fight for justice for other exonerees and continue to be amazed by her strength.

Kristine is my hero, she is my Miss America, and most importantly, she is my sister. She chose to be there for me. At the lowest times in my life, she was the one to comfort me and then tell me to "put on my big girl panties" and deal with it. She is my longest unbroken relationship. She has never waived from her commitment to me. The grace that she has shown, even at her darkest moments, has helped mold me into the woman I am today. From the moment I was freed, I have tried to make her proud of me.

She taught me at a young age to be strong in the worst of circumstances, even if you are broken. Her grace and love for others taught me to have a kind heart. Respect was earned; not something that everyone deserved. I learned that life wasn't fair and that you had to roll with the punches.

She also taught me values and morals. She was my biggest defender, yet she handled me privately when I had done wrong. She understood that I was a young girl who was being unfairly thrown into an adult system. She treated me as a child and gradually allowed me to grow into a woman.

I wish our justice system was fixed. The sad truth is the American justice system is broken. We need to demand more from our politicians and judicial system leaders to fix it. Together, we must demand that another Kristine Bunch case doesn't happen. We should protect each other from a broken system.

No matter how hard I try, I could never fully understand the pain that she has endured over the last twenty years. Writing her story has been the biggest honor I have received and the biggest challenge that I have ever faced.

Kristine's journey has taught me so much. I never dreamed that I would write a book that would change my life in so many ways. Although I was there for her during her journey, writing her story was more painful than I ever could have imagined. I learned more from her. I know why I have always called her Miss America—she has shown me how to survive the worst of circumstances.

I am honored to be the person that she chose to write her story, a story filled with heartbreak and pain. Her journey will inspire you, as it has many others. Let me take you on the journey that she had to walk, and continues to walk today.

Chapter One: Small town

Kristine Bunch was born a small-town girl to her parents, Arthur and Susan Bunch, on October 5, 1973. She was born into a small-farm community near Connersville, Indiana where her parents lived on the land of Susan's parents. Kristine's grandparents had long built a small empire which included a bakery and two farms, along with her grandfather being a design engineer. Her grandparents were financially secure where her own parents struggled to make ends meets. Kristine recalls her early childhood as happy and she felt loved especially by her grandparents, whom she was close to growing up.

The farm had chickens, cows, fields for planting, a barn and a pond. Lazy days were spent fishing in that pond. The farm seemed like the biggest place in the world. Of course, it was work too. Cows would get out and would have to be steered back into the pasture. It was frightening to be so little and have those big animals headed your way.

On the other side of the pond was an orchard. Kristine loved to sneak through the fence and curl up under a tree to munch on an apple. It was a special hiding spot and one that was filled with treats. Wisps of sunlight trickled through the branches making it seem like a magical place. Kristine was always imagining fairies hiding in the cool shade and munching on apples.

In 1977, Kristine got a little brother to love. Anthony Michael Bunch was born October 6, just one day after Kristine turned four, a birthday gift that she may not have enjoyed much in her youth. Over the years, that bond between a brother and sister was the strongest connection that she had. She loved her new role as big sister. It wasn't hard for Kristine to develop this bond as Michael was easy to love. Michael was never called Anthony. He liked to eat so everyone started calling him Mikey...after the commercial that says, "Give it to Mikey, he will eat anything."

Kristine entered kindergarten and she was already ahead of most her classmates. She loved to read and was even known to read Shakespeare at a young age. She enjoyed school and was eager to learn as much as she could. She loved to write and allowed her imagination to guide her pencil into beautiful pieces of work, earning her a young author's award in fourth grade.

Winning the award would have made any parent beam with pride, however after her father called it a hobby, Kristine stopped writing. She heard her father dismiss her achievement as nothing more than a necessary past time, not as a potential career. It was the first of many disappointments that would follow.

Kristine doesn't remember her parents having an easy time of it. Kristine's dad was a welder. When he worked, the pay was steady. However, there were many layoffs. When he wasn't working, he had a full-time job with the farm. Kristine's mother worked in the bakery. It was a tough life, but Kristine remembers it being happy. She adored her dad.

With both parents working, Kristine started watching Mike

at a very young age. The big joke is how Mike could drink Worcestershire sauce straight from the bottle. Kristine was so little that she thought it was cough syrup because it tasted bad. Anytime Mike had a cough, he received a dose. To this day both kids can eat Spaghetti O's and vegetables straight from the can because Kristine wasn't big enough to use the stove.

There was so much pressure to grow up. From this point on, Kristine was a caretaker. They were on their own often and had to take care of each other. Many normal childhood things were put on the backburner because the kids had to watch out for each other. It is a relationship that was cemented, no matter how much they fought, and would stay as strong throughout their lives.

Kristine's parents divorced while she was in fifth grade and soon she would be faced with new challenges. At Everton Elementary school, she was an exceptional student who was ranked in the top 20% of students in the state. She excelled in advanced classes and was challenged by her teachers. She had friends whom she had bonded with over their years at the elementary school together. Her life was good and she was on the track to excellence in middle school.

During her 6th grade, her mother moved Michael and Kristine to another small town, Greensburg, Indiana. They left the comfort of the farm that her grandparents owned and the life that she was used to. Any move can be stressful, however this move changed everything for Kristine. She lost the regular contact that she had with her grandparents and other family members who surrounded her. She was in a new town and she struggled to make friends. Her school work was too easy and she could easily have tuned out the stuff that she knew because there was no challenge for her anymore. She was becoming increasingly depressed. Kristine no longer loved school, often skipping to go fishing with her little brother or to stay home to watch T.V. Not that the school nor her parents addressed the missing days. Kristine was forced to raise herself and Michael. Her world that she had known was quickly crumbling. Her parents' divorce changed the way she saw the world. It also took away their dad, who didn't want to make the 45-minute drive so, he was no longer getting them on the weekends.

Divorce took a toll on Kristine's sense of relationships, she had watched her grandparents who were still 'young in love.' It was a forever commitment that she saw with her grandparents and she thought that her parents should have tried harder. Kristine and Michael should have held them together; she wondered why that wasn't enough. It was something that she could understand and she hurt.

Susan bought a trailer in Greensburg near Lake McCoy, in the Creswood Resort trailer park, which was outside the city and literally, out in the boonies. Lake McCoy was a dream that was created by Carrie McCoy in 1905 and evolved over the decades, becoming a popular tourist attraction in the 1930s. The trailer was walking distance from Lake McCoy.

While Kristine struggled to make sense of her new town,

her mother soon made new friends and to make matters worse, her mother, at the age of 28, married a man 10 years younger than herself. That was a low blow for Kristine. She was angry that her mother didn't see the mere four years' age difference between Kristine and her new husband as an issue. She was angry that this boy was her step-father. It worsened their relationship and made Kristine even more distant from her mother. She felt that her mother wasn't looking at what was best for Michael and herself, but rather her own happiness.

Throughout her depression, Kristine was still focus on Michael and trying to give a better existence than she felt. She was devoted to him and tried to encourage him to be better. She was lost inside this new world without any real goals. She decided that she was done with school and dropped out before she even entered 9th grade. No one even tried to stop her.

A high school dropout hanging out with friends, Kristine began to smoke and drink. She was living her own life. She was looking for anything that brought her joy, even if it wasn't the normal things that teenagers did. The stage had long been set for Kristine to be on her own with the little supervision and bad judgement set by her parents, she was just following their example.

During the midst of her mother's relationship, there was one relationship that would change Kristine. Susan met Tom Claxton when Kristine was 14. Tom was a neighbor at the trailer park who worked in a factory and would soon set boundaries with Kristine and Michael. He gave them some much needed structure, such as curfews, with the attachment of strong love. He would give her a quarter just in case she needed to call for anything. He was a father figure to Kristine and someone who changed her life forever. There was a mutual trust and love. Even when the relationship between Tom and Susan failed, he stayed in Kristine's life. It was a relationship that would last the rest of Tom's life.

At the age of 17, finding out she was pregnant was a surprise for Kristine who had been on birth control pills for years. She thought that she had the worst flu ever and that it was lasting for months. After learning of the pregnancy, Susan supported her daughter, advising others that she wasn't the first and wouldn't be the last. Tom also vowed to be there for her too.

Knowing that she would need her G.E.D. so that she could get a good paying job, she quickly got her G.E.D. It was the first step to providing a good life for her unborn son. With Tom's help by letting her rent one of his trailers, she was on her way to being stable. She also got two-part time jobs: one at auto parts store and the other was at Kmart where she could use her discounts for toys and clothes. Kristine was looking forward to being able to provide for her son. She felt stable and grounded. She knew that she was going to give him a good life and she was willing to work as hard as she needed to do that.

The father of her unborn son was unready to make a commitment to Kristine - not that she wanted that - she didn't want to get married just because she was pregnant. She was willing to be in a relationship with him; just not a marriage. She knew that she wanted that commitment to be more than just a shared child. Five months into her pregnancy, he walked away from her and his unborn child, making the final decision easier for her. She never waivered and continued to work towards her dream of being a good mother to her son. She knew that they would be okay.

Kristine was young and was about to be a teen mom. It changed everything for her. She went to work and school trying to give him a better life. She wanted everything to be perfect for her son. The months leading up to his birth, she was already planning on giving everything that she could. She wanted to be the best mom to her son. He wasn't planned, but she welcomed the surprise that he would bring to her life.

Chapter Two: Tony's life

Kristine had to be induced. Labor did not start on its own. Once labor started, it was obvious that something was wrong. Kristine's pelvic bone wasn't shifting the way it was supposed to. She wasn't dilating and each time a contraction hit the baby came down and hit the pelvic bone. The doctor quickly decided that she couldn't give birth naturally and an emergency cesarean section was performed.

Anthony Maxwell Bunch was born March 11, 1992, making Kristine Bunch a single teen mother at the age of 18. His middle name came from her mother's brother who was tragically killed in a car wreck before she was born. It was a tribute for her mother.

From the beginning, Kristine saw the blessing that God had given her. Tony was a sweet baby who slept through the night and stole his momma's heart from the first moment she laid eyes on him. Kristine never saw the struggles that she faced as a burden or a sacrifice, only as a choice that she made to ensure that Tony would have the best life possible.

Kristine worked two jobs to help as she juggled the bills and spent every moment with her son. She doesn't being recall being a stressed-out mother, after all she had a support team that was helping in the raising of her young son. The daily routine was having breakfast together, taking a bath together, heading to Tom's (Tom was Tony's babysitter - Kristine didn't trust anyone else) and off to work she would go. When work was finished, Kristine would pick up Tony and head home. Tony helped while she made dinner, did laundry and dishes. After dinner, they would play Nintendo, watch movies, or read a book.

Each year for Tony's birthday, Kristine would blow up hundreds of balloons to tie up on the ceiling. During his party, she would drop the balloons on him. At first everyone said that it would scare him. Instead, Tony threw back his head and laughed.

On June 30, 1995, Kristine woke up. She remembers that it was foggy and it took her a minute to grasp what was happening.

She rushed to get her son through a wall of fire. Her only thought was getting to her son. When she saw the flames, she looked for the fire extinguisher that she had. Unable to find it, she tried to throw a blanket on the flames. That blanket went up in smoke causing her to leave the trailer in search of help. She went outside, screaming for help, not sure how to get to her son but determined to save him. She broke the window with a tricycle to get to her son. Tom would later testify that when the window broke, the room became engulfed with flames. When Kristine tried to climb into the window, someone said that it was too late and that he was gone. In a matter of seconds, her life that she loved was gone.

Chapter Three: Charged with Murder

In the morning hours of June 30, after the flames were extinguished, Kristine was sitting in an ambulance waiting for news of her son. She asked her neighbor Tom if they had found Tony, still believing that he was alive. In her mind, she had survived and he would too, never be imaging the worst was coming. She was hurting by the loss of her trailer and thinking about how she would start over. With her head hurting and feeling like she was in a daze of confusion, she was waiting for news about her son. She couldn't imagine a world that didn't include her son.

However, she could not save her son and was taken to the local hospital for an examination. There, she would be given a Xanax to try to calm the grieving mother. Her injuries included cuts and blisters, but she was also covered in soot from the fire, even coughing up black phlegm at the hospital. However, she wasn't treated or even tested for carbon monoxide poisoning.

The investigators from the Indiana State Fire Marshal's spent an hour and a half investigating the scene of the fire and went to the hospital before she was even put in a hospital room. At 10:30 that morning, she had a two-hour interview with police in her hospital room. There officers told her that it was arson and someone had poured gasoline in their house to try to murder them. She was released around 5:30 p.m. with medication to help her sleep. She returned to Tom's trailer to rest; she had to deal with her new reality... she had lost everything.

Around 10 p.m., the detectives asked Kristine to come to the police station to answer a few questions. Having lost all her belongings in the fire, she went barefoot and unprepared for what she was walking into. She was faced with unimaginable grief and trying to answer the questions of detectives surrounding the fire that destroyed her trailer.

Between trying to properly bury her only son, she was also faced with detectives asking all the questions that she had no answers for. She wanted to help the detectives, even though she was at a loss for who would want to set fire to her trailer, let alone who would want to harm her or her son. She had no list of suspects to give to the police detectives. In her mind, her life was simple - she had no enemies or could ever imagine a scenario that would make someone want to set fire to her home. She left that night feeling more lost and confused, even telling her mom that she didn't want to be alone with the detectives again. The detectives asked her about life insurance and home owner's insurance. They kept saying she must have had a reason. Kristine explained that she didn't even have insurance on her car. Her son was 3 and she didn't think that she needed life insurance.

From the start of their investigation, fire marshals and detectives questioned Kristine Bunch as a suspect, rather than a grieving mother. Even as Kristine was saying her good-byes to her son they were building a case against the young 21-year-old mother.

Kristine returned to the sheriff's department to answer detectives' questions determined to help in any way that she could. She was raised to believe in law enforcement and if you tell the truth, then you will not be in trouble. She had nothing to hide and wanted justice for her son, if someone had deliberately set fire to the trailer. There was little sleep for her in those beginning days, she was consumed with loss and now she was pondering who could have set fire to her trailer.

Along with questions for Kristine, they asked her to take a lie detector test and she readily agreed. She was strapped into a chair with her back turned to the man conducting the test. Having never had a polygraph she was unaware of the different techniques that would be employed by him, such as the way he would lower his voice, or how he would raise it to try to intimidate the suspect. She remembers feeling scared by his yelling and not being able to see his face only made it feel scarier.

The polygraph process was another thing in her life that felt like a blur. She was a walking zombie due to the Xanax that she was given to try to deal with the loss of her son. Coupled with the lack of sleep and food since those simple tasks were too much for her. The moments that she could sleep were plagued by nightmares of the fire and she could hear her son calling for her and she was searching for her little boy. Waking to her reality that her boy was gone and that her life would never be the same; she was living without her reason for living. The only life that she had known and loved was gone. She was living her American dream and it was Tony that had given her that peace. She was a mother - that was her prized job. She had lived to be his mother and now she was a mother without her son. Her world felt different and now she was facing this screaming man.

After the polygraph, the polygraphist informed her that she had failed. He told her that he knew that she was a monster who had murdered her son. On July 5, 1995, just five days after the fire, Decatur County Sheriff's Department deputies placed Kristine under arrest for arson and murder. Along with the failed lie detector test, one of the fire investigators believed that Kristine had deliberately blocked the door of Tony's bedroom. He said that a chair was obstructing the door way. They also had a fire report saying that the fire was arson. There were also conflicting statements from others alleging that Kristine had said that someone was in the trailer. In addition, the detectives claimed when asked why she did this, she had replied "I don't know." The detectives charged her with two counts: arson and murder.

Before the era of social media, most people got their news from the nightly news or newspapers. In the months leading up to Kristine's trial, the case of Susan Smith was highly publicized. To investigators, they had another Susan Smith on their hands. On October 25, 1994, Susan Smith told the investigators that a black man hijacked her car with her two young sons in the backseat. For nine days, the nation felt the pain of Smith's tears as the 23-year old mother pleaded for her son's release. They watched as the unimaginable was happening to Smith.

After a few days, Smith admitted that she rolled her 1990 Mazda into the John D. Long Lake in South Carolina. She said there was no motive or plan to do it - however it is believed that she did it to be in a relationship with a man that did want the boys. The Susan Smith case changed the way that police investigate crimes involving the death of children. Motives were no longer needed when dealing with cases involving mothers. It changed the way, Americans saw mothers accused of such crimes. It was no longer unacceptable to believe that a mother could kill their children in cold blood. The thought was if one mother could kill her children with no motive or financial gain, then others probably could do it too. Her case changed the minds of potential jurors.

Unlike Susan Smith, in Kristine's case there was no motive. There was no reason that Kristine had to want her son dead. She had a support system to help her with Tony as she worked and her every free moment was spent with him. She was a loving and dedicated mother to Tony. There was no life insurance on Tony and Kristine didn't even have life insurance for herself. There was no man in her life who didn't want children. There was no motive to support the detectives believing that she was the cause of the fire.

However, there was evidence. The ATF ruled the fire arson. Per the ATF forensic chemist William Kinard, there was a presence of Heavy Petroleum Distillates (HPDs) in samples that were collected by fire investigators Bryan Frank and James Skaggs during their investigation. They believed that they had found pour patterns that were consistent with a fire or arson. They had concluded quickly that the fire had to be deliberately set.

Kristine was sent to the Decatur County Jail - a place that she had never been. The Decatur County Jail was located at 119 E. Railroad St. A jail that has been built in 1979 and just a 10-minute drive from Kristine's trailer. Although she was 10 minutes away from her old life, she felt miles away. She was engulfed in a world that she had never been in.

Jail officials worried that Kristine would try to commit suicide and placed her in a single cell where she was under constant monitoring. She was unfamiliar with the legal system, as she had never been in trouble with the law, not even a traffic ticket. She was thrown into a cell with no real expectations of what was happening to her. She was in the beginning stages of her grief. Her grief was replaced with feelings of being confused and lost.

Her new surroundings were filled with grey walls, a toilet, and a metal sink along with one mattress that was placed on a metal platform that would serve as her new bed. Her life was destroyed and now she was forced to sleep on a metal bed. It felt as if her world was crashing and she was helpless to understand. To make matters worse, sleep was impossible to achieve now. She was already sleep derived from the fire and now this metal bed was more than she could bear. She was locked up facing charges in her son's death. Kristine had no understanding of how this was happening to her.

All of Kristine's material belongings were gone, but her everything was gone: her son. Her arms ached to hold her son and to breathe in his scent, anything to feel the greatest love that she had ever known. She was dead inside. Her reason for changing her life around years ago was gone, the reason that she was working long hours in the factory in hopes of giving her son a better life than she had. Now she had nothing and she was in an unfamiliar place with no understanding how this nightmare was happening to her. Her reality had dramatically changed within a week. One Wednesday night, she was fixing dinner for Tony and the next week she was being fed through a metal slot in the door, trying to make sense of her tragic circumstances. It was a daunting task.

In October 1995, Kristine's lawyer got her a bond hearing. Her request was going to be heard by Judge John Westhafer. His first job out of college in 1964 was as a corporate lawyer, but his desire to serve Decatur County brought him to serve as a judge. Westhafer had been one of two judges for Decatur County since 1977. This was not his first murder trial. One of the trials that he had presided over was the trial of Stuart Kennedy who kidnapped and murdered a young woman. For that crime, Judge Westhafer sentenced him to death, which was later overturned by the

Indiana Supreme Court.

Judge John Westhafer granted Kristine a $50,000 bond, which required a $5,000 cash bond for her release. At the bond hearing, the judge found that she was not a flight risk and there was a lack of motive. After the conditions of her bond were met, Kristine was released to her mother on October 12. Her trial date was set for November 28.

Being out on bond did not make dealing with Tony's death any easier. Kristine was still facing a murder trial and fighting for her freedom. She was fighting for justice, even if that justice was clouded with suspicion of murder. Along with all her grief, she was faced with the judgement of others. People would stop and stare while making comments, such as "There is that woman that killed her son." In this small town, their suspicions became her problem as well. She had to deal with local gossip if she left her home. She couldn't even go to the store without hearing comments or feeling the stares.

On Halloween night, looking for a way to forget her reality that was filled with loss, she went to a bar with her mother. Her mother quickly matched Kristine up with a stranger and although she wasn't looking for a relationship, and after too many drinks, she escaped her reality with a one-night stand.

In early December, Kristine learned that she was pregnant again. A surprise at best, after being told that she may experience problems becoming pregnant after Tony. It was the first time that she had felt real joy since the fire. She had a purpose again. She knew that she had to go to trial to fight for her life and that she could not take a plea bargain. She had to be there to raise her child. Her baby needed a mother and she needed this miracle baby. She knew that that this baby could never replace Tony, however, she still had the love of a mother to give. She knew that she could love this baby as much as she did Tony. This baby was a miracle to her just as Tony had been. Her children were her reason for living and gave her life purpose. She may not have understood the process of the trial, but she knew why she was fighting. She had to fight to be there for her unborn child.

Before trial, the prosecutor offered a plea deal to Kristine: plead guilty to the arson and the murder charge would be dropped. In exchange, she would receive a 15-year sentence. Although she was unfamiliar with the judicial system, she knew that she could not pled guilty to a crime that she did not commit. She believed that any jury would see the truth and she would be set free. She chose to go to trial to defend her innocence.

The day before her trial, the local paper printed an article that said that Kristine had failed a lie detector test and that she made statements of guilt during the police interrogations. In small towns, the feel of the community is often the same as the local media. Small towns are clouded by single views, views that are loosely based on gossip or the word of the law enforcement. She would face a trial by her local peers who were likely influenced by small town gossip. Gossip that would be stronger since murder didn't happen every day in Greensburg.

The question about who told the local media about the polygraph is unclear. However, the intention is clear, the article painted an ugly picture of this mother who was on trial for the murder of her son. There was not a reason to publish the story and it only led to more suspicion for Kristine's case. The polygraph results had no place in a local newspaper article. It should have been argued in court instead.

Polygraphs are rarely used in court; this test is used by police to determine whether a suspect is guilty. You see it all the time on crime shows where the detectives know from the minute a suspect fails a polygraph, that they are guilty. There was no mention of Kristine's lie detector test by the prosecutor in her trial, only in the media.

The statements that were published by the media were also questionable. Again, those statements should have not been published prior to trial but instead should have been argued in the courtroom. The statements and the lie detector results could have been used to taint a jury into believing that Kristine was guilty prior to trial - an unfair move if it was done by the prosecutor, or simply bad journalism on part of the writer of the article. In the 1990s, with the lack of objective journalism that we see today - largely due to the different social media pages - it was common for local media to write based on the views of the prosecutor. The article was one-sided and it would not help Kristine's chance at a fair trial.

Chapter Four: Five days in Hell

Kristine's lawyer was unprepared. Her state-appointed attorney, Frank Hamilton, had never defended a murder trial in his 20 years' experience, 12 of those years as a deputy prosecutor for Decatur County. He had no experience in preparing his client for trial either. From the start of the trial, Hamilton advised Kristine to show no emotion, that the jury would see tears as admittance of guilt. She was five months pregnant and fighting for her life and for her son's memory. Kristine headed to trial to prove her innocence and to finally tell the truth. Kristine felt confident that she would be acquitted of all charges and that the truth would set her free. She believed in the legal system and that innocent people do not go to prison.

Kristine's lack of experience with the court system and its process did hurt her. She was left to trust her fate to the lawyer that the state had provided for her. She was unaware of how jurors looked at the public defender and the lack of emotion could have seemed heartless to them. She trusted that her lawyer would make the jury see that she was innocent and that the evidence, while it did suggest arson, did not point to her. She was forced to sit there and listen to the arguments of guilt and innocence, waiting for the truth to be clear. She was innocent. She had to look at the crime photos and listen to the details of Tony's death. The tears were not flowing on the outside; however, she was dying on the inside. Her whole world was crushing and all she could do was rub her stomach touching her unborn son and pray. She believed in her innocence.

The prosecutor for the state was William Smith. Smith started his career as a private practice lawyer in Greensburg in 1973 and had worked in the prosecutor's office since 1986. This wasn't his first murder case either and one of his cases was also surrounded with doubt. That case was State of Indiana vs. Larry Howard Biehl. Biehl was accused of killing one teenager and injuring another teenager boy. He won a conviction against Biehl, even when the defendant's mental capacity was questioned.

Along with his mental capacity being in question, the crime itself had some questions. However, Smith still tried the case as a first-degree murder.

Although Kristine was unfamiliar with the legal system, she knew she had to listen to the trial and she was hoping that the jury would see the truth. Her lawyer told her that the jury was looking for reasonable doubt and any negative emotions would help them convict. Without a display of emotion and her lack of understanding of the judicial system, her chances for a fair trial was looking grim. She was lost in her grief and now facing a life sentence, her only concern was for her unborn baby. Her life and her unborn baby's life were in the hands of the jury as opening statements began.

In opening statements, Smith told the jury that he would prove that the fire that killed young Tony was arson. He also said that he didn't need to prove that there was a motive for the crime. He would show them how even Kristine's inconsistent stories would prove her guilt. He claimed that there were two blazes set in the trailer that early morning - one in the living room and the other in the southwest bedroom that Tony slept in. He also told the jury that Kristine had even obstructed the door of Tony's room by putting a recliner chair in front of it.

Without the ATF report, the case, State of Indiana v. Kristine Bunch, was a circumstantial case with no motive. In Indiana, it is not necessary for the prosecutor to prove a motive to the jury. A motive was not necessary as a motive is not always known, but if a prosecutor has the evidence to prove a crime, a trial can proceed. Smith laid out his belief that there was a motive; Kristine simply didn't want the pressures of being a young mother. Tony was an obstacle to the young 21-year-old mother. He painted a picture of an unhappy mother and the fire was just an end to that unhappy life.

In his opening statement to the jury, the defense attorney, Frank Hamilton, said he would prove that no fair investigation was done. The investigation centered too quickly on the fire being arson and the fire investigators didn't consider it to be anything but arson. It has been said that the first 48 hours of a police investigation are the most crucial to solving a crime. During those 48 hours, police and fire investigators were solely focused on Kristine. There wasn't a focus on anything but arson and the only survivor. He also pointed out that Kristine was a loving mother who gained nothing by her son's death. Unlike the prosecutor, he told them that she was a devoted mother who was committed to raising Tony with a promise of a better life. There was no motive because she didn't set the fire. She was innocent.

The state called Bryan Frank, a fire investigator who was on the scene of the fire. He told the jury about the burn patterns that were shaped in a V shape. Those patterns led him to believe the fire was deliberately set. He told them that the fire was started in the living room and the southwest bedroom where Tony slept. It was unusual that the fire was drawn down and in his experience that only happened when an accelerant is used. He also advised the jury that special tools were used to determine the presence of accelerants, including a trained canine.

Another important witness for the state's case was William Kinard, the forensic lab chemist who tested 10 samples taken from the fire scene. He testified that five samples - one from the south bedroom and the other four from the living room - tested positive for HPD, or accelerants. His final ATF report was entered in as evidence against Kristine.

The ATF report was the most damaging piece of evidence against Kristine. His report would haunt her for years to come. Even as she listened, emotionless to his testimony, her doubts about the fire were there. She just couldn't figure out who could have done this to her and especially to her son. If the report was correct, Kristine thought, then who set her trailer on fire and why hadn't she seen them that morning. It was a constant torture for her and made her wonder if she could trust anyone at all.

Ron Clark, a fire fighter, who had gone into the trailer in search of Tony, testified that he had to step over the chair. He also stated that he had to climb over an obstacle just to get to Tony's room. He noted the presence of the recliner chair blocking the door.

The state also called several witnesses who told of inconsistent statements that Kristine had given throughout the investigation. A neighbor had testified that in the early morning hours after the fire, Kristine had told her that Tony was locked inside his room. This couldn't have been true since that door had been removed before the night of the fire.

Connie Land, the trailer park manager, testified that a week after the fire, Kristine and her mother returned to the park to thank people for their support. During that visit, she claimed that Kristine told her that someone else was in the trailer that night and had sprinkled her and her son with either gasoline or kerosene. Land also testified that Kristine did not appear to be acting like a grieving mother and seemed as if nothing bad had happened.

The state also questioned Kristine's injuries, calling them minor and inconsistent with direct contact with a fire. He also questioned her different accounts of the night of the fire, such as where Tony had fallen asleep. He calls into question whether she had seen or heard Tony that night, or if she woke up to the smoke. However, the state did not mention any test findings on those injuries. There was no mention of doctors or EMTs who could have determined the level of Carbon Monoxide in her system or even a detailed look at her "minor" injuries. An unprepared jury wouldn't have known the importance of this missing evidence.

When the defense opened, the case was weak in comparison to the state's version. He called few witnesses and Kristine was not on that list. The decision not to call Kristine was based on whether he believed she could handle cross-examination by the prosecutor, something that wouldn't have been easy to handle for the young, grieving mother. Kristine did not object to his suggestion to her taking the stand, as she didn't have anything to add to the case that wasn't being covered by the witnesses. She simply didn't know who could have set fire to her home.

One of the witnesses was a private investigator, Tom Hulse, who disagreed about the cause of the fire. It was his opinion that it could have been electric, since there had been evidence of past electronic problems in the trailer. He also stated that it should have been ruled undetermined, not arson. He said that fire investigators rushed to the conclusion of arson too soon and did not take time to investigate other reasons behind the fire. The rush to judgment likely affected their conclusion towards the only survivor of the fire, Kristine.

Relatives and friends took the stand to testify about the relationship between Kristine and Tony. One friend spoke of Kristine and Tony as having a great relationship. "He worships her and she worship him," she said. Another friend spoke of the rumor that Kristine had asked her to take custody of Tony just a year before. She explained that she did not say that to the police but that the police had told her that they had heard the rumor from other sources. She denied the claim and said that during a hard time Kristine had asked her if she would raise Tony if something happened to her. She said that it wasn't an offer of custody. She refuted half of the things that investigators were claiming during her statement. She reinforced that Kristine was a loving and great mother to Tony.

Kristine's mother, Susan, told the jury that the chair that Ron Clark said was blocking the door wasn't. In fact, it was there so it would not obstruct the heating vent. She admitted that it did stick out a little, but not as much as the state claimed. The chair had always been there and Tony moved freely around it. She also told the jury that Kristine couldn't have trapped Tony in the room since the door had been removed before the fire. Another thing that she tried to clear up for the jury was the manager's testimony about Kristine's words at the trailer park. She was with Kristine that day and she never heard Kristine speak, let alone say anything about the fire. She testified that Kristine was still in a state of shock due the loss of her son; that she was barely speaking to anyone let alone talking about the morning of the fire.

She could shed light on why the manager, Connie Land, would lie. Susan and Land were in litigation following the fire and there were hard feelings between the two women. She implied for the jury that Land's testimony was not reliable due to the litigation.

Kristine did not take the stand in her own defense. Hamilton felt that Kristine would not be a good witness. He also advised her throughout the trial to remain emotionless as the jury could take her emotions wrong. As she sat there, five months pregnant and listened to all the evidence, she felt lost and confused. The evidence of the ATF report hit her the hardest. She had always believed in science and that report was solid facts. Yet as hard as she tried, she couldn't think of one person who would do this to her. During the trial, Kristine never cried but inside she was dying. The level of grief and confusion that she felt was overwhelming. However, she had to keep fighting; her unborn son needed her to fight. She had to listen and pray that the jury would see the truth or at least reasonable doubt.

Kristine struggled with the evidence, knowing it looked

very convincing. However, she knew that it couldn't have been her and she did not see how this was happening to her. Just a year earlier, she was working at temporary jobs and taking welding classes so she could provide a stable life for Tony and herself. As she sat there listening, the only place that she could go to in her mind was her memories of her son - which were now being clouded by the attack against her. She was angry that anyone could think that she would ever harm her son. She was still angry that she couldn't save him that morning. Her grief was impacted by hearing the details of the trial. She was not sleeping in the nights of the trial, as she faced every moment thinking about the worst-case scenario - life in prison. She was scared for her life and now her unborn child who was the only thing that she felt that she had left.

Closing arguments begun with the prosecutor, William Smith, who reinforced the state's theory of the fire and Kristine's possible motive, since he was not required to offer a clear motive. He said that even though her friend said under oath that she never spoke of giving Tony up, he still believed that was the motive for the fire. He told the jury again about the chair blocking the 3-year old's door. He didn't want the jurors to forget about all the inconsistencies in her story and the many things that she spoke in the days after the fire. He also did not want them to forget about the ATF report that proved it was arson, which caused the death of young Tony.

Kristine had to sit there and listen to Smith, trying to hold it together but inside she was broken. She felt dead inside and wanted to scream out in pain. Her hands rested on her stomach as she prayed for strength and for the jurors to see that she was innocent. Her pain continued to mount throughout the trial, however, in the closing arguments, she was truly broken.

With closing arguments made, the jury was released to determine Kristine's fate. As Kristine was led out of the court with her father, she wondered if these were her last free moments, or would the jury see reasonable doubt setting her free from the nightmare that left her in a fog. While she waited for the verdict, her father and Tom got her coffee from the gas station and she chain-smoked as she waited. She couldn't go anywhere due to the stares and whispers, something that she couldn't handle.

It took the jury five hours to convict Kristine of arson and murder. As she listened to the words "guilty, guilty" on both counts, she thought her ears were deceiving her and couldn't grasp the verdict. Her shock turned to disbelief. Kristine couldn't believe that they said guilty. She honestly did not believe that things could go so wrong. She sat there listening to their recommendation against a life sentence, instead for a set number of years with the chance for her to have a life afterwards. In her shock and disbelief, all she could think about was what kind of life would she have. It didn't register until she was put back in cuffs and was headed back to the jail.

At her sentencing, less than a month from the verdict being read, Judge Westhafer sentenced Kristine to 60 years for the murder and 50 years for the arson - to be served concurrently. The Judge didn't mince words - he accused Kristine of getting pregnant again to gain sympathy from the jurors and promised her that she would never raise that child. He threatened that the baby would become a ward of the state and she would never see the baby.

Kristine heard the sentences of 50 and 60 years and nothing else. Her mind was spinning and the thought of 110 years was her life. She would die in prison and they were going to take her child away from her. The past nine months hit her all at that moment as she tried to understand what was happening to this small-town girl's life. She had never felt so hopeless in her life and now the State of Indiana seemed to have control her life. It was traumatic for Kristine and she was forced to listen without understanding why it had happened. Her life was over and there was no one who could help her. The tears flowed as she struggled to hear the judge's words, she was stunned and beyond shocked by the sentence. All she could think about was her unborn son and what was best for him. Her nightmare had just become her reality.

Chapter Five: Welcome to Indiana Women's Prison (IWP)

Kristine Bunch was transferred to Indiana Women's Prison (IWP), the first and oldest women's prison in Indiana, established in 1873, located on 401 Randolph Dr., in Indianapolis, on April 1, 1996. I.W.P., a maximum-security prison, was located in downtown Indianapolis and could hold 420 women. It had special dorms that specialized in mental illnesses, longer sentences, and pregnancies.

Kristine was greeted by old buildings and circles of barbed wire, a 110-sentence looming over her and the new life growing inside of her. She had to stay healthy for the sake of her unborn son and learn the ways of the prison to survive. She entered at the age of 21 with the release date of 2026, which would make her 53 and her son, 30. She entered the prison thinking that she would die there and that she had lost everything. She was carrying a child that she wasn't even sure if she would get to raise. She felt lost and was hurting beyond normal standards. The move to the prison was done quickly, due to fact that the local county jail wasn't equipped with a doctor that specialized in pregnant women. She was moved the same day as her sentencing; April Fool's day.

Kristine was placed in the intake dorm of the prison. Pregnant women were dressed in blue uniforms so they are easily identified from the other inmates and kept away from the general population inmates. Indiana Women's Intake (IWI) was a dorm that set up within IWP to access each inmate and determine the best place to house the prisoner. For Kristine, that decision was likely made within days, she was pregnant and had a sentence of more than 40 years. Both meant that she would remain at the IWP rather than being transferred to another women's prison.

During her time in intake, Kristine needed to talk to someone about the enormous amount of pain she was in. She was broken by her loss of Tony and the past 9 months of being accused and eventually convicted of killing her precious boy made it difficult to cope with daily life. She was lost in her grief, lost in all the emotions that she could not express as she felt that it was all too much to handle. There was no understanding of her pain and being in prison only made her pain magnified.

She wrote Superintendent Dana Blank and told her that she needed someone to talk to. She also told Blank that she was innocent and that she was overwhelmed by her new circumstances. She knew she couldn't wait for the prison psychologists, who already had a full load. Blank responded with help and Kristine began to speak to a staff member twice a week.

IWP was set up differently than other Indiana prisons, mainly because of the superintendent. Blank took over the role in 1991, when the prison was believed to one of the worst women adult prison. She was known to say that "you are not your crime" and she believed in reform. Her beliefs led to the restoration of education programs and making the prisoners personally responsible while they were still behind prison walls. She believed that the prisoners still needed to be accountable and that programs were needed to make them ready for society again.

Blank did not run a prison that focused on the crime, but the person. She believed that inmates still needed to have some dignity while incarcerated.

Blank allowed the inmates to wear their own clothes instead of uniforms; each inmate was allowed 30 items of clothes, 6 pairs of shoes, and a limited number of accessories. Inmates were held to higher accountability, which is why she allowed some luxuries, such as jewelry, for the inmates. She believed that she was helping inmates prepare for life outside of the prison.

Kristine was placed in a dorm that was named the "Lifers Dorm," a term given because of their sentences being 40 years or more. The dorm was equipped to hold 40 women and was set up differently than the rest of the prison. Each inmate had their own cell that is closed off from other inmates. Each cell has a single bed, a locker, and a small desk with a metal window that either looks out on the prison yards or the alley of North Hamilton, Indianapolis. Being a lifer also meant that Kristine would get an annual picnic, where family members can come in with food from the outside.

From the start of her sentence, Kristine couldn't accept her verdict or her sentence. Her innocence would not allow her to adjust to prison. She couldn't accept the sentence. Her survival was dependent on how to learn to hide her feelings or her weakness. She couldn't allow herself to be vulnerable, as weakness would make others view you as prey inside the walls of I.W.P.

Walking into the prison, Kristine was pregnant with her son. How she got to this place was beyond her understanding. With both boys, her life was changed. Tony changed her life by making her change her lifestyle and focus on the future. Kristine believed that God was punishing her when she lost Tony, being blessed with Trent made her realize that God hadn't punished her. In fact, he gave her the one thing that would keep her focused and fighting.

Kristine quickly met Mariah who helped her adjust to life

behind prison walls. Their friendship would make the transition to being prisoner DOC #966069 a little less traumatic. Kristine had to adjust to prison life as an expectant mother, knowing that she would likely have to give her son up. There wasn't much to feel hopeful about and her first few months were spent focusing on taking care of herself and her unborn son. She was walking around feeling the loss of one son while trying to be as healthy as possible for her unborn son. She was breaking more by the second and she wasn't sure how she was going to survive this hell.

One of the first things that Kristine did was go to the prison's law library to find out if the judge could take her son as he had promised at sentencing. The thought of losing her child was heartbreaking and terrifying and even with her sentence, she knew that she couldn't bear the pain of losing another child. The law clerks quickly assured her that she could determine who would take her baby from the hospital and that they could help her with the paperwork. It was a small blessing that she found comfort in.

Through the shock and her grief, Kristine went through everyday life as a prisoner and she would have to learn to adapt to her new surroundings. Every prisoner had a job classification. Since Kristine was pregnant, her options were limited. She was assigned to be a G.E.D. tutor, which paid a $1.30 day. There she would assist other prisoners who were studying to take their G.E.D. test. The job offered little distraction from her sentence, however, it did keep her from crying in the bed all day. In her job, she could focus solely on helping others. She helped others achieve their G.E.D., for many leading to their immediate release, something that Kristine couldn't do. She was happy that she could help, yet the pain of her circumstances was overwhelming.

There are no special arrangements made for prisoners that are expecting except for a nightly snack given to the mothers as they went through the dinner line. It was usually a milk and peanut butter and jelly sandwich, nothing like the cravings that expectant mothers could experience. She was blessed to be able to buy snacks from commissary, however her biggest craving was to be free. There were days that she struggled to eat due to her grief. Her pregnancy was already hard, but it was made worse by being an inmate. She was in constant pain from her 2-inch mattress and she had bad feet pain, which Mariah would try to massage away. The biggest pain was when she would feel her son move around, knowing that she would soon have to give him up. She cried herself to sleep where she at least might dream of a different future than she was facing. The hours not sleeping were spent worrying that she wouldn't get out to raise her sweet boy.

Learning to adjust to the prison was different for every inmate. I have heard some prisoners say they treated it as a college experience and even one that it was like boot camp in the army. There is no true adjustment for the innocent though - there was always a part of Kristine that knew she shouldn't be there. She knew the cost of her freedom was simply being stole from her and her unborn son. There was no way she would ever fully adjust to prison life, that would have meant that she would have to accept her sentence, something that was impossible for her.

For Kristine, she wasn't a typical prisoner. She didn't come into the prison with a bad attitude or lack of respect for authorities. She knew that it wasn't the prison officials fault that she was there and that they were there to do a job. Her attitude helped her adjust to the prison as much as possible. Kristine didn't mind having a schedule, it helped her not to focus on her pain and grief. She knew she had to find a place that she could fight her conviction, even if she didn't know where to start.

The months went on and the closer that her due date approached, Kristine's fears grew. She only felt strong enough to handle this because of Trent, a name picked out by Mariah. Soon she would have to give him to her father until her release would come. The more that her son grew inside, the more her fears were realized. She had to remind herself that she would be there to raise him and that she had to have faith, even if that was all that she had. The physical pain of her pregnancy held no comparison to the shattering agony that she was feeling. She could hide the tears behind a smile that lied to the world. When the lights went out, the tears soaked her pillow as she tried to

sleep.

Chapter Six: A Promise with Empty Arms

Grief has no direct path for dealing with loss nor does it have an easy way to handle loss. Kristine had to deal with her grief inside a prison while carrying her unborn son. She fought every day to deal with the loss of Tony, her beautiful boy who was taken from her far too soon. She also had to deal with the fact that with every passing day she was carrying her son who she would have to say goodbye to him as well. She knew that soon he would leave her body in delivery and instead of being put into her loving arms, she would have to give him up too. The amount of grief was soon going to be doubled. Her loss of her sons would be her biggest challenge and her greatest burden. She woke up every morning praying that Trent wouldn't be born today, so she could be with him one more day.

Kristine's grief was the cornerstone for the fight for her freedom. Somehow, she had to deal with her loss and the future loss of her other son. She allowed herself to get lost in the daily routine of being a G.E.D. tutor - where she was a helper to those who needed the help and the routine helped to ease the pain a little. It didn't take the edge off the pain though. The distraction didn't even scratch the surface. However, Kristine had to keep telling others that she was fine and even speaking those words "I'm fine," was making her pain worse.

All of Kristine's life, she was above her circumstances and she was in control of herself, even when her circumstances were full of misery. She believed that she could build a better life for her and Tony. Now, a year later, she was going to have to deliver her baby and give him up too. No amount of courage prepared her for the battle that she was in for.

On July 22, 1996, after failing to hear a heartbeat, Kristine Bunch was rushed to Wishard's Hospital to have an emergency C-section. Trenton Michael Bunch was born in a hospital room full of locks while his mother was shackled to the bed. After a brief stay, Kristine was forced to hand over her son, but not before Kristine whispered to her newborn baby, "I will make it home to you before you are 18." A mother's promise that would prove to be the beginning of the fight for her release.

Kristine was released from the hospital the day after Trent's birth and quickly returned to the prison where her father had arrived with her newborn. She spent the next two hours holding her son and wishing that she could take him home instead of handing him back to her father. The pain was more than the physical pain that she was experiencing. Her grief was taking over as she held Trent close to her trying to breathe in his scent and remember his every feature.

According to Parents magazine, "the normal recovery time for cesarean surgery is six weeks"[2] and that is a in a home environment - not a prison environment. She was sent back to her cell on bed rest as she tried to heal, but also deal with the loss of her son. As a new mom, her arms ached to hold her son or to see him sleep. The moments of being able to get lost in his sleep as he moved around, or to be the one that comforted him when he

---

[2] A. (2016, December 04). Your C-Section Recovery: Timeline and Tips. Retrieved April 2017 rom//www.parents.com/pregnancy/givingbirth/cesarean/c-section-recovery-timeline-tips/

woke up fussy were stolen from her. Some women experience postpartum depression - this felt worse than that for Kristine.

She didn't have her son to hold when she was sad, only the few pictures of him taking in the first few days which were no doubt outdated as he was growing rapidly. There were never enough pictures that could be taken to show his life to this grieving mother. She was physically healing, however her emotional health was fading as she was forced to watch her son grow beyond the fences.

The months that followed Trent's birth were unbearable for Kristine. She had given temporary custody to her father Arthur and her stepmother, a decision at the time she felt was the best for Trent. She had little contact with her newborn for the first six months of his life. Her visits with Trent were few and too long apart. Too many days came and went without contact and she was quickly becoming more depressed, lost in the background. She had to wait for her father or stepmother to bring him to see her. The few visits that she did have happened when her mother would go get Trent. Even when visits were regular, they could only be 10 hours of visits per month. During the visits with her son, she got as many pictures as she could. She would hold him close and cry when she had to hand him back. The walk back to her dorm was painful as every step she took she was getting further away from her son, further into a depression that clouded her life. Her arms were empty and her heart was broken.

August saw the start of a friendship that would change Kristine's life. Kristine met a fellow prisoner who was close to Mariah, a young teenager struggling to find her place inside of the prison. Kristine met me, a lost 15-year-old serving a 25-year sentence for arson, which resulted in the death of my mother and sister. I needed someone to hang out with after Mariah returned to college classes and Kristine happily agreed, not knowing what to expect.

Kristine did not know much about me, but knew that Mariah loved this "baby." Mariah treated me as a child without making me feel that way. Kristine spent a few nights at REC with me and immediately saw what Mariah saw - a baby thrown away from the system. I had no real support and was housed in a special needs dorm. It was a dorm that housed prisoners with severe mental illnesses and knew nothing about how a young teenager should be treated. I was more comfortable with Mariah and now Kristine was looking to help her as well.

In August of 1996, Kristine also quickly took advantage, of a program that she was not eligible to take while pregnant. The cosmetology program was an 18-month vocational program that offered a six-month time cut, but it would also give Kristine a new skill. The program was a viciously demanding program that meant she would have daily homework followed by morning tests. She credits that course and her teacher for learning better study skills, skills that she tried hopelessly to teach me, as I was struggling with high school courses. She could immerse herself into this world of learning, taking her away from the hell she was living. It required Kristine to focus on her studies and less on her prison sentence that would not have been affected by the time cut, as her sentence was decades away and the mere six-month time cut would not have changed her sentence. Her reason for taking the classes was to learn a new trade and have something good come from her sentence.

Kristine liked to stay as busy as she could. Between taking her classes and her commitment to me, she was overwhelmed. However, with all the things that she juggled, there wasn't a moment that her pain was gone. She was trying to raise her son and fight the guilty verdict that had her sentenced to 60 years. It was like she was living but not breathing. She could see the birds fly into the prison and wonder when she could fly away. She was waiting for the chance to see the truth revealed, that she was innocent. She believed that her sentence would have been easier to do if she would have been guilty - at least then there wouldn't be an injustice. But she was innocent and stuck in a frightening prison that she didn't know how to escape.

Kristine wore that fake smile as a badge, but not as a badge of honor but simply because she had to. There were moments that she was forced to be another version of herself. Pain does that to a person. The person she was before could never imagine living inside a cage where you had to be searched before and after visits. She didn't have to imagine having to allow her belongings searched at any time. She had no rights and little understanding of her sentence. She knew that she had to find a way to fight her conviction. She was waiting for the Indiana State Public Defenders office to start her appeal - a standard request.

Kristine's father, Arthur, had the legal custody of Trent following his birth. However, Susan, Kristine's mother would still go visit her grandson. During one of those visits, she over-heard Arthur's wife talking to Trent while feeding the young baby. Susan heard her say "Eat for mommy." Susan was quick to speak up and correct her that Kristine was the only mother that Trent would call mommy. For Kristine, hearing of this conversation, it was worse than being slapped in the face. She wanted to be the one who spoke those words as she fed her son. The fact that someone was trying to take that away from her was heartbreaking and made her everyday pain greater. She already feared that her bond with Trent would weaken the longer that she was away from him. She rarely saw Trent in his first six months and now she was faced with someone encouraging her son to call him mom, instead of grandma or nana. Her pain was turning into anger over her situation. She was losing more every day and the worst loss were her sons, one living and another that she couldn't grieve for properly. It was unbearable for her to watch everyone else raise her son.

After Susan, informed Kristine of this conversation, Kristine went to the prison's law library to change the legal guardian from Arthur to Susan. She knew that she was not going to be replaced in Trent's life before she even had a chance to be his mother. She also had the commitment of regular visits with her mother who had already been visiting regularly without Trent. It gave a little hope for more time with the baby boy who she missed more every day.

Even when the weekly visits become a regular thing, two

hours or less were too short. She longed to hold him at night by his crib and sing to him as she had with Tony. She left every visit in tears waiting for her next visit. It was a pain that was only worsening. Her son was growing and changing while she was stuck inside the prison. She would leave the visitation room wishing for more time, instead of having to watch her baby grow up on the other side of the barb- wire fences. Her losses were quickly stacking up against her and with every day there was new pain.

The pain that Kristine felt over the loss of raising Trent was unbearable. She couldn't tell anyone about her feelings and bottled them up inside. She was living but she was dying with each new story about his daily life. She was jealous to the point that she that she felt she hated her family. She was missing his first words and the first time he sat up. She was having to watch him grow up through someone else's eyes. She wondered if she made the right decision by allowing her family to raise him instead of giving him up. With adoption, she wouldn't have to see him grow up without her beyond the fence.

February 1997, brought some joy for Kristine and her now 6-month-old son. The Indiana Women's Prison opened the Family Preservation Center. The new center would allow prisoners to have two hours a week with their children without other family. The set up resembled a preschool environment with cribs, bean bags, and even a comfortable couch. It had toys for all ages of children and was set up to be homier for the inmates. It was just for the mom and their children. There wasn't even an officer present in the room, just the center employee. It was a more normal environment for the children and gave the moms a chance to have more of a one-on one relationship with their children.

Kristine looked forward to her visits and they helped to hold her together. The Family Preservation Center also gave her more strength to hold on. During her regular visits, she had to listen to her mother when she just wanted to talk with her growing toddler. In the Family Preservation Center, they could run and play. She could lay on a couch and they could take a nap together. She could watch her sweet little boy sleep and when he awoke she was there to help him wake fully with her kisses and hugs. Those visits were the most special that they had together. Those visits gave her a strength to fight. Her love for her toddler was her glue that held her together when she was away from him. She knew that she had to find a way home to him.

Kristine loved every visit in this home-like environment, where she could focus all her attention on Trent. For those two hours, she didn't feel the pain of her reality and could just be the mother that she longed to be. She could cuddle on the couch with her sleeping son and hold him as he dreamed in his baby land. It was a couple of hours that she could pretend that they weren't separated by her harsh sentence. She could be a mother to her son without hearing others. Her only focus was on this beautiful boy. Opening that center was a huge blessing for Kristine and other mothers.

When Trent was a young toddler, he went fishing with Kristine's dad, Arthur, and fell, causing an open wound that required four stitches. This event caused her tremendous guilt because she was not able to be there for him. She couldn't be there to console him or to hold his hand through the procedure. She couldn't take him for ice cream afterwards and tell him what a big boy he was. It was just another injustice that Kristine had to deal with.

Change was a battle daily for the women at I.W.P., having no control meant that you had to always be prepared for change. The more that my lawsuit continued through the media, the Department of Corrections realized that I.W.P. needed a dorm that was set up to deal with younger prisoners and formed the "Youthful Offenders" dorm. It was dorm set up for offenders 25 or younger.

This new dorm meant that Kristine's dorm, "Lifers," was no longer a dorm. The 40 women were quickly reclassified to other dorms. Even though Kristine was only 24, the dorm was only set up for 20 inmates and at that time, there was enough prisoners under her to fill the beds. She was classified to MSC - a dorm that held 180 women in six different dorms. The move meant that she no longer had her own room. Now her bed was a bunk bed in a shared cubicle. She now had a "Bunkie," another prisoner that would sleep below or above her. Her locker was in a row of four and she had to lock it to protect her belongings. In the Lifers dorm, there was a mutual respect among the prisoners, but now she was among the open population. Her prison life was completely turned upside down by the move.

The move to MSC put Kristine in a more vulnerable and uncomfortable position. She used to be able to rest in the quietness of her single cell and now she had to hope that other inmates would respect others by being quiet. During the day, it was next to impossible to get quiet. At night, she had to learn to deal with the bed hopping, the art of going over lockers and beds to reach their lovers. She was surrounded by new inmates, some who had spent more time on the inside than on the outside. She had struggled to understand the prison from her single cell, but now it was even harder to understand. She knew most women from her daily interactions, but living with them was a new challenge.

Kristine tried to maintain civil relationships, however that would be harder in this new environment. Drug dealers and petty crimes like check fraud seemed to give those women the right to judge. She kept her head up, but she had to learn to tune out the negativity - not an easy thing to do when you have nowhere to hide. She had to defend her crime, even though it wasn't her crime. It was heartbreaking to hear others say that she was a baby killer, or even make statements about bad mothers that she knew were directed towards her. It made her keep her guard up even more than before. She was surrounded by women that had no respect for others and most didn't even respect the law, which was proven by their repeat trips back to the prison. It was ironic to her that her new cell mates were more prisoners than the lifer's dorm, where it had been a close-knit group that were more civil to each other. Most had short sentences which should have meant that they would be better prisoners than someone who had nothing to lose by causing trouble. She had no understanding of why these women did not value their freedom and just kept coming back to the prison.

In May 1997, Kristine was moved to the Youthful Offenders Dorm, where Mariah and I were living. It was the first time that she had lived with her baby and it reunited her with Mariah. The dorm was smaller than MSC and although it was still an open space, she felt some comfort by being around her friends. Kristine believed that this move was a chance for her to say goodbye to her baby, me.

I had recently won her lawsuit and things were looking good for me to be moved to a juvenile treatment center. It was a move that would benefit the 16-year-old teenager who needed the therapy. Their relationship wasn't lost to the prison officials, as they could see the power of their friendship. They knew that Kristine could calm me and help me get through daily life. She was happy to be able to spoil her baby and we both knew that the day would come when we would have to say goodbye.

I remember the day that she moved up to the dorm, I had just returned from my high school classes and saw her a few beds down. Beyond excited, I yelled down to get her attention and she immediately turned around, stopping her conversation with someone else and said, "Hi baby." Seeing her made my upcoming move easier. However, it was still extremely hard for me. Kristine had become more than a friend, she was my sister. Kristine reassured me that she would make it through and that the center would love "her baby."

Every day was a chance for Kristine to make me stronger and prepare me for the move. It was a great move that the prison made and it probably helped me say my goodbyes to Kristine. Every day I was blessed by her wisdom and strength as she tried to prepare me for a new experience. She would make me different treats like ice cream, all while telling me that it was all going to work out. She tried to prepare me for the center and dealing with teenagers again. She told me that I was still required to be on my best behavior while telling me to have fun too. She wanted me to grow stronger, knowing that I would be getting the help that I needed. Having Kristine there to help me prepare me for the hardest part of my sentence was a gift, she was there to encourage me when my fears become too great. She tucked me in to bed every night and prayed over me for sweet dreams. She was also there to check me when my attitude got bigger than me. She knew how to calm me and build me up stronger.

June 9, 1997, Kristine learned that her baby was gone. Prison officials had quietly packed my things after everyone went to their morning assignments. However, true to prison gossip, messages got to Kristine that I was gone. She was thankful that she went to breakfast with me that morning, something that I didn't do unless it was waffles or pancakes - my favorite prison breakfast. We had spent the morning together and Kristine even made me my favorite coffee. Although hugs were against the prison's policy, we hugged every day. Her last hug with me was around 7:45 a.m., after protest from me since I was trying to go back to sleep. Even though she knew that I had been moved, walking past my bed was difficult. Kristine looked at the empty bed knowing that she had seen her baby possibly for the last time. Who knew what the future held for either of them, one of us could be released by the time I turned 18, when it was expected that I would have to return to the prison.

The uncertainty of my whereabouts crossed her mind, since it wasn't released to the media until after I arrived at Crossroads in Fort Wayne, Indiana. Kristine wanted to believe that I was safe. She tried to believe that I was in a better environment, but she worried about who was going to rub my head when I couldn't sleep, or who would be there when I had one of my many breakdowns. Her heart hurt and she felt yet one more loss. She felt as if she just lost another baby. She couldn't explain their bond, but it helped them both and now I was gone. Just another loss that her wrongful conviction created and something that she was getting used to.

After my move, Kristine was quickly moved back to MSC and her comfort was gone. Her move back to MSC was expected and she was determined to not feel the agony that she felt before going to the Youthful Offenders Dorm. She had to become a little stronger and perhaps a little colder too. She knew that the units of MSC had a level of coldness that you have learn to accept. There were many different areas of the prison and each held a different hell that she had to learn to deal with.

Being in MSC, you had to be prepared to fight at any moment, or protect your stuff more. Even in the Youthful Offenders Dorm, you could leave an item on your bed without fearing that it was going to be stolen. The smaller group of women respected each other, or at least as far as "prison code" went. In MSC, there was such a high turnover and continuous moves within the dorms that the respect couldn't be built collectively. It was a dog-eat-dog environment and that meant you were on your own. Relationships were built over time however, but with all the incoming and outgoing of inmates it was hard to maintain trust.

Chapter Seven: Becoming Miss America

Kristine Bunch was struggling in a prison with the label "baby killer" and with no help from the legal system. The judicial system isn't set up to help the innocent. For years, Kristine was left to rebuild her life and considering that she was in a prison that would be the challenge of her life. How was she supposed to live in an environment that was filled with murderers, drug dealers, or even other innocent women? This was the harsh circumstances that Kristine was faced with.

Kristine quickly learned that the prison wouldn't protect her, as she was just one of 400 women. There were threats against her and she had to defend herself from other prisoners who viewed her as a monster. She had to learn how to survive inside walls that had no concern with safety, or even if you ever walk out. The guards were there to do a job, not to save lives. It was a world that Kristine had never known and now she was forced to learn how to live.

Kristine's choice was simple. She knew that she was innocent and she would fight, even if she was unsure where to start. The choice to keep fighting meant finding acceptance with her current sentence. Kristine had to become a prisoner to survive. That didn't mean that she would ride out her sentence without a fight in the court system. Her injustice didn't make her want to fight against the prison officers. She always believed that it was not their fault, they were just doing a job. It meant that she would continue to fight the unjust sentence, but she would be a productive prisoner. She would have to learn how to survive this without losing herself too. Even in the moments that she felt the weakest, she never wanted to disrespect others. She was respectable of the rules, even some of them that made no sense to her, as an innocent woman. She would learn to live with the conditions.

Kristine had every freedom taken from her. The right to raise her son was the biggest thing that was taken. However, every day that she wasn't allowed to leave, she was losing the right to form relationships, get a job, sleep in a real bed, the list is longer than words could describe, and she lost everything. Kristine felt lost and angry. Throughout the months that were growing into years, there were moments that she didn't think she could fight anymore. Thankfully she was committed to raising her son. That was her reason to keep fighting.

The doubt they put in Kristine Bunch's mind surrounding Tony's death was unbearable. Thoughts that consumed her daily had a profound effect on her and kept her up at night. When the lights went out, Kristine was forced to lay on her bunk and wonder. She wondered who could have hated her so much that they would set her home on fire? Did someone have a grudge against someone in her family? Although there were doubts that consumed her, she never wavered about her innocence. She knew that she could never admit to a crime that she could have never committed. Her innocence and her love for her son, Trenton, would have to save her sanity. It would be the driving force to bring her home. She would prove her innocence and she would do it as gracefully as Miss America does when she walks across the stage shortly after winning the title.

Loss is such a profound emotion that it can break a person or it can make a person soar into a better life. It can bring one to their knees and at that moment, they crumble, losing all sense of reality. For some, like Kristine, they refuse to give into the feeling of loss. She didn't have the chance to stop and grieve her loss of Tony. She was forced to fight for the right to be the mother that her newborn son Trent needed and deserved.

Kristine quickly learned the number one rule of prison; you must watch out for #1 – yourself. She still maintained that compassionate attitude and did nice things for other prisoners, especially the expectant mothers. She would give them food or advice, as she knew the pain of being pregnant while locked up. However, she also had to be cold to some people who tried to run games on her. In prison, you should be careful who you trust something that Kristine had never seen before and it changed her in ways that she still can't understand. The game of prison life influenced the way she viewed people and she couldn't understand how some people could be so heartless with a normal appearance.

She learned how to be social but not best friends with everyone. She gave respect and expected the same back. Although she wasn't a problem inmate, she knew her way around the rules of prison.

Even though Kristine knew that she did not set the fire that she was convicted of, she still felt guilty. As a mother, the number one job that she felt she had was that she was supposed to protect him. She felt that she had failed to save him. She blamed herself for leaving him in the trailer when she ran out to get help. She knew that she was trying to save him, however the pain that she felt because she couldn't save him was excruciating. The daily guilt that she carried was more than most could bear. She struggled to get through everyday life without falling apart. Her guilt, she came to know, was considered survivor's guilt and was completely understandable.

The American Heritage Dictionary defines survivor's guilt as "A deep sense of guilt, combined often with feelings of numbness and loss of interest in life, felt by those who survived some catastrophe. It was first noticed among survivors of the Holocaust. Survivors often feel that they did not do enough to save those who died or that they are unworthy relative to the perished."[3]

Survivor's guilt can be caused when someone lives and someone else dies. It can happen when someone survives a plane crash or even a house fire. Survivor's guilt is a normal response to a trauma that Kristine suffered through. Even if Kristine would have never been prosecuted, it is likely that she would have still suffered from survivor's guilt. A mother's job is to protect their

---

[3] (survivor guilt. (n.d.). The American Heritage® New Dictionary of Cultural Literacy, Third Edition. Retrieved November 7, 2016 from Dictionary.com website http://www.dictionary.com/browse/survivor-guilt)

children from harm, even the harm that is unseen or cannot be avoided.

The effects of survivor's guilt can last for years. Kristine could not begin the process of dealing with her grief and prison was not trained well enough to deal with her. There were grief programs, however even in those groups they promote acceptance of guilt to properly to start the grief process. The counselors who ran the groups meant well, they just were not able to host a grief group for the innocent. This was their job, they worked inside a prison with the guilty. Not exactly the place that people are expected to be innocent. Kristine was in programs that were geared towards rehabilitation of prisoners and remorse was a huge part of their success. They were preparing the prisoner for potential parole hearings or sentence modifications where release is almost always centered on showing remorse from the accused. Kristine would leave some of the groups feeling defeated and vowing not to return. She was tired of feeling judged by others who didn't believe she was innocent or feeling like she had to hold back due to the fear of judgement. She learned that not everyone is someone who she could talk to about her truth.

Kristine needed intensive treatment - treatment that would help her deal with her guilt and her PTSD. PTSD, or Post Traumatic Stress Disorder can happen to anyone that goes through a traumatic event. The death of her son due to a fire was the cause of the traumatic event, however her conviction and sentence were also traumatic experiences. Every day that she was spending behind lock and key was an injustice and she was feeling more anguish, and so very alone. She was feeling like she couldn't breathe even when she had to. Her world would never be the same and she was less of a person than she knew before. The Kristine Bunch who was sentenced on April 1, 1996 was fading and becoming another person, even if she didn't want to.

Kristine enrolled in college classes offered by Ball State University in August 1997. She had always love to challenge her brain, learning new things, especially in literature, which was a passion. She took as many English classes that she could. She found herself drawn to the Iliad and the Odyssey. She could relate to Homer and the concept of heroism. His words about the honor system and the struggle of believing in your honor spoke to Kristine's belief that the system would do the right thing by her. She could get lost in the different concepts that centered around the right thing to do. She could focus on her studies and got lost in a world where justice was real.

With a full college schedule, Monday through Friday for three hours a night, she would hold as many three jobs at the same time within the prison to pass the time. She never allowed the sentence to control her. It wasn't her sentence, just another reminder of the injustice that she was facing. She tried to stay as busy as she could, hoping the pain would lessen. She couldn't sleep anyway and at least she could make extra money.

Although I was still in the juvenile treatment center, Kristine could have limited contact with me. After a letter was discovered through the mail, Kristine was called to Ms. Blank's office to discuss the matter. Kristine expected to be warned about the illegal contact. Kristine believed that they understood the bond that she shared with me, as I didn't have any family to support me. In many ways, Kristine was all that I had. Instead, she was advised that she could write one letter a week and would be allowed one from me as well. It is unclear whether they knew that she was also calling me twice a week. If they knew they never addressed the calls.

The reason that the prison would allow this contact is unknown - perhaps Blank knew that I needed Kristine. It was evident before I left, the impact that Kristine had had on my life. My behavior was calmer and outbursts were minimal. She found comfort in taking care of others, especially me. I was young and naïve, yet she saw something in me from the moment she met me. It was love that Kristine still had to give and maybe in both of our grief, we found comfort. It was unthinkable to think that prison could cause such a bond, but with me she found someone who needed to be loved. She found someone who needed her love- love that she still had to give.

Kristine struggled to understand her conviction, especially being surrounded by inmates that readily admitted their guilt. One of the reasons that Kristine was so close to Mariah was her honesty and it allowed them to have a friendship that would survive the walls and fences of prison. Mariah was there to comfort Kristine in those dark days and that mattered more than any crime that Mariah could have committed. With little hope with her legal case, Mariah and I gave Kristine a peace that it could work out.

In 1997, Kristine received some hope when she learned that her case was being appealed. State Public Defender Eugene Hollander was assigned to the case. The appeal was challenging the jury instructions and whether the jury had received the proper instruction on the motive evidence and the circumstantial evidence. It questioned whether there was evidence to support the murder conviction. It also challenged the conviction of felony murder and if it was included in the arson charges. The appeal asked if the sentence was too harsh.

Kristine received a standard letter from the Public Defender that was assigned to the case. She never met him face-to-face during the process. He advised her not to get her hopes up without offering her clear answers on the process. Even after another lawyer had scammed Kristine's family out of money with claims that he would assist with the appeal, Kristine still believed that the appeal would set her free. She still believed that the judicial system worked for those who told the truth. She believed that she would be freed. She still believed in the way the system worked.

Chapter Eight: Murder Upheld

On June 9, 1998, the Supreme Court vacated the arson charge, citing that "a person cannot be sentenced for both a felony murder and the underlying felony."[4] It was double jeopardy for Kristine to be convicted of arson and murder. This decision meant that she was now just convicted of murder with the 60-year sentence, not changing anything for Kristine's release date. Although, the courts ordered Decatur County to vacate the sentence, it was still on their record.

Kristine didn't receive a phone call from her state public defender, instead she received it in her nighty mail. As she struggled to understand the language in the written verdict, she was feeling the lowest since her nightmare began almost three years to the date.

Losing this appeal crushed her hopes and dreams of freedom. It would have been easy to stop fighting and serve her

---

[4] Bunch v. Indiana. Supreme Court of Appeals. 9 June 1998. N.p., n.d. Web.

sentence, praying that she would live until her outdate. It was an end to her fight with the assistance of the Public Defender's office, as they do not carry the case to the Supreme Court. As far as the State of Indiana was concerned, the case was closed.

Although there wasn't anything more to do with the appeal, Kristine didn't lose her will to keep fighting. She still had a reason to fight. She didn't lose everything! A reason to keep asking the courts to reverse her sentence. Her reason was her son. He was the reason that she kept fighting, even when the pain was so great that Kristine could barely wake in the mornings. She had to show him that the system could get it right by granting her freedom.

Kristine woke the next morning and focused on her life as it was. She wasn't giving up, but she had to find a way to live, even if that meant inside these fences. She wasn't going to lie down as much as she wanted to. She had to find a way to survive.

Kristine was lost in the system. Her daily routine included

college courses and a full-time job. Her hours were spent trying to figure out how to get another trial and due to her inexperience with the laws, she was basically having to listen to the advice of other inmates. Every prison has jailhouse lawyers, who research every part of the law trying to find ways to fight their conviction, or simply find a loophole in the laws. Whether the inmate is right or wrong, it is best to listen to their rambling since something might help.

Prison lawyers are usually the ones that have either been in and out of the prison systems, however the good ones are the ones that have spent all their years researching their cases. They find different cases that could help them win a new appeal. A lawyer is needed of course. They spent their time looking for any loopholes that could get a conviction overturned, even if they knew that person was guilty. The different theories that Kristine had heard about other cases did interest her, but she had no clue where to begin her own research. She had read her court files and didn't see a smoking gun in her own case. She knew that she was innocent but was clueless on how to prove it to the courts. She listened to everything thinking that maybe one day it might be useful.

As quickly as her son was growing, there was no progress in her legal case. The decision to vacate the murder charge happened in 1998, but since then nothing had been filed. The years were becoming harder with no movement on her case and no clue where to start. She had little resources or knowledge to gain her freedom. There wasn't any money to get a lawyer to help navigate the conviction. By 1999, she had begun to feel hopeless in. As much as she wanted justice and her freedom, she was still prisoner #966096.

With each passing year, she was left to worry if she would be ever freed from the nightmare that was her life. She graduated from cosmetology in 1999, where she stayed on as a tutor for her teacher Mrs. Lewis, who she had become close to as the years passed on. She loved her job and worked harder than anyone else. She also took a third shift cleaning job to pass time and earn an extra $0.65 cents a day. Her routine was set and it helped to fill the sleepless nights. She would spend Monday through Friday with a full schedule, then sleep on the weekends between visits and maybe a meal or two a day. She was literally watching her life vanish more every day, as her son was growing too fast to keep up with through pictures.

Kristine was also working along with Mariah as a Lay Advocate in the prison's program, a program that had inmates being advocates for other prisoners against written discipline action. She took the position to help other prisoners fight their new pending write-ups. She enjoyed the program and she was well educated, making her a good addition to the program. However, it had its drawbacks, since it was her against the same officers and staff that she was expected to listen to.

Kristine knew that she was innocent, but she wasn't living in the real world. She was living life as an inmate. She was forced to play a game inside I.W.P. Most prisoners couldn't care less about guilt or innocence, it is simply a game of survival. The more power that you held, the better you succeed. To beat the system was a feat that Kristine didn't know how to do, but she knew how to make her time bearable.

Kristine surrounded herself with few, but was respected by many. She didn't trust many, but she never disrespected others either. She knew how to get what she wanted by turning on her charm. Hers was a charm that she learned from being a prisoner. She knew that her innocence didn't mean much to others, as most prisoners say, "But I am innocent." She couldn't let others see her pain, as that would have been a weakness. A weakness that could allow her to be taken advantage of and would have allowed someone else to control the only freedom left to her. She was barely holding herself together and living this life was making her feel older than her early twenties.

Kristine was missing out on the normal lessons that most women learn in their 20s. There is no age in prison. You are forced to be older and wiser, it is the only way that she knew she could survive. Where she had no understanding for the people that surrounded her, she went through her daily life as there were no worries. She held the weight of her conviction like a 500-pound weight on her shoulders and there was only way to survive - to act natural. Well, prison natural.

The mind of a prisoner varies from prisoner to prisoner, but it is all the same. There are some prisoners that own their crimes and use them as a threat to others. However, Kristine found out soon that no one cared about her innocence only how "tough' you projected yourself to be. She had to become someone that even she didn't want to be. She had to be that prisoner that had no remorse. It is only something that you can understand when you have been locked up and disregarded. She would have never believed that she would have to become the prisoner that she was. It was a game that she had to play. With no hope of a release date, she was fighting to maintain whatever sanity was left inside her.

Being that prisoner was tougher than any other role she had ever known. She was locked up, everything that she ever known was taken and her children were gone. Trent may have been alive but she was still missing every crucial moment of his life. The tears couldn't flow, she couldn't run, nor could she hide, she was simply stuck in this nightmare.

August 1999, brought a familiar face back to Kristine. I, was returning to the prison to finish my sentence. It was a day that Kristine had waited for and yet dreaded also. She had hoped that I would be released after going to the treatment center, however I still had seven years left of my sentence. She was determined to be there for me and help me readjust to the prison life again.

Waiting by the officer's desk in the educational building, Kristine smiled brightly as I walked through the door and immediately rushed to her, falling into her arms with tears flowing. It was a connection that was still the same as it had been for the last two years. Kristine knew that her schedule just became busier with my return, but she also had her baby again, so she was ready to sleep less if that is what it took. She gave me my favorite snacks, pop and nutty bars and one last hug before going to our classes. Something was right in this horrible place.

My return did give her comfort, however it also added to her schedule as I, who was still young, wanted as much time as possible. I was demanding and Kristine struggled to keep up with her already busy schedule and trying to research her case without knowing where to start. However, she knew that I needed her help to readjust and even when I played games for attention, Kristine was there to stand her ground with me. Her only concern was to help me find my way again.

A little older now, I struggled to readjust. Working and college courses were different than I was used to at the treatment center. Kristine never gave up on me, even when taking care of me was exhausting. She knew that I needed her. Putting her own pain aside, she listened for hours as I complained about everything and after a few months, told me to grow up. She used tough love on me and it worked. She got me to see her situation for what it was. "You have an outdate that is in this same decade, but you have got to work for it." It was the start of a more grown-up relationship between us.

Kristine always believed that I could succeed. Kristine knew that I was a fighter and as much as Kristine wanted to give me everything, she also knew that she had to start the preparation for my homecoming. It was something that Kristine wished that she was doing, to be on the other side of the fence. Despite that, Kristine would help me start looking at the future, a future that wasn't in prison. Kristine put all the energy that she could into making me believe in myself. Kristine knew that I could succeed if she toughened me up a little. She used a classic tool: tough love. It was painful for her to be tougher on me, but she knew that she couldn't watch her baby in this prison anymore. Kristine showed her loyalty to me by preparing me for the real world, when Kristine could have simply let me make the stupid mistakes that most youthful offenders make after release. Kristine knew that I could succeed even if she couldn't be there to guide me as she had done for me inside the walls of the prison.

The lessons of life that Kristine was teaching to me were lessons that she would have likely shared with Trent also. Kristine was a natural mother who had lost her sons but still had that love to give. She was born to be a mother. Her personal experiences made her stronger and helping people was her natural talent. She was a great friend who offered compassion and wisdom to her "peeps," people who may not be family by blood but by loyalty, which meant more to her. The lessons of life that she taught made the difference in many lives.

There was little to be hopeful for Kristine, however she always had faith. She went to church and felt a sense of peace while attending services. In 2000, she began the steps to convert to Catholicism, after having found something that she had never experienced before. She found a peace even within the walls, almost like she was feeling God's love for the first time. With the help from the church, Kristine began taking education classes about the values of the Catholic Church, the history and the beliefs. She also learned about the proper order of the celebration of mass. Kristine's new faith gave her comfort that she had never experienced before. She knew the meaning of love, but now she knew what true love was. Her faith would be tested throughout the years; however, it was also strengthening when she relied on her faith that God would see her through. Her attitude that God doesn't make mistakes helped her prepare for the long fight that she was facing. It was a comfort that no person could ever give her.

With her newfound religion, Kristine found another way to pray. She began to ask God to show her the way that she could help herself. She had been waiting years for someone to rescue her from this living nightmare where sleep was worse than being awake. The amount of pain that she had to pretend wasn't there was overwhelming her inside. She found comfort in praying and found comfort in her faith.

Kristine also attended a weekend-long ministry weekend called "Kairos." A nationwide ministry that goes inside the prison for a weekend retreat, Kairos provides inmates a different experience with religion. It is geared towards all areas of religion and volunteers from different religious backgrounds assist inmates in finding God, even in the prison. It was a profound weekend for Kristine and for the first time in her incarceration, she felt no judgement. The volunteers weren't there for guilt or innocence, only for souls that needed to feel God's love. The ministry would come back monthly to be with the inmates and continued to be a support for the inmates. This is where Kristine met Betsy Marks, someone who would help Kristine beyond the fences.

It is only normal to find happiness, whatever way that she could. Kristine worked a job as a warehouse worker, a job that she had earned due to good behavior. Her job was to unload trucks next to the fence and as a standard procedure an officer had to be present since it was close to an exit to the outside world. The officer that was normally posted there was a good man who treated Kristine with compassion.

The relationship between Kristine and Mr. Piquant[5]

started out as a normal friendship, just as it could have if Kristine wasn't an inmate. Mr. Piquant was a warm and friendly guy that loved life. They could talk about their sons and the different struggles that they both faced. He may have been a free man, but he was still denied his rights to his son. The pain and reasons may have been different; however, it was still pain that they both could relate to. That bond and connection caused normal progression of romantic feelings for Kristine. She may not have been in love with him, but she had feelings for him.

The relationship lasted for over a year and had Kristine not been locked up, it would have been her longest relationship. Mr. Piquant was kind and gentle to her. He treated her as a human being, not inmate #966069. More importantly, he treated her as a woman. Attraction lead to desires, which lead to sexual passions. It was illegal for this relationship to occur, but it was a beautiful thing. They led this secret life and for those stolen moments, Kristine felt passion. She felt that she was something other than a

---

[5] (name changed to protect identity)

convicted felon. It gave her a release that was trapped inside her for years.

As careful as they were, a year into their relationship the truth was discovered. Kristine was placed in lockdown for the first time since her incarnation at I.W.P. Her new cell was an 8 x 12 room that had a desk, bed, and a slot in the door for food exchange. There were some cells that had a toilet, but the prison officials wanted to make an example out of Kristine, which is why they put her on the side that had no toilet. She found it demeaning to ask the guards every time that she had to go to the restroom, but she wasn't about to let them see that weakness. They even moved her cell to the back of the building facing the alley of North Hamilton Street after she was accused of sending messages from her window facing the prison. The only messages that she sent was the hand motions of hearts and "I love you" to her friends, especially me. She knew that simple act was against the rules, but that was her family and as much as she needed them to know that she was okay, it was something that she needed too.

The investigation started after a staff member said that they walked into the warehouse and felt like they had interrupted something between Kristine and Ofc. Piquant. Another inmate signed a statement that she witnessed Ofc. Piquant coming out zipping his pants and Kristine wiping her mouth. After 12 days in lockup, Kristine was given a polygraph, which she was answered the question "did you give the officer a blowjob?" She answered no and the results were conclusive that she was telling the truth. She wasn't lying either, the inmate got the details of the encounter wrong, it was the other way around. Just another way that Kristine viewed the relationship with Mr. Piquant - she was the one who got the pleasure. She held to her belief that she was worthy of pleasure too.

By passing the lie detector test, Kristine was released from lockdown, barely in time to save her college education, but not before she lost her annual picnic. The annual picnic was a rare event that allowed her four hours of family time and enjoying a meal together. After the investigation, she was released back to open population having to be moved to another dorm and different job classification. While she didn't face any new charges for the affair, her life was inconvenienced yet again. She quickly got back into the swing of open population, even getting her job detail changed to something that she wanted. Not that the prison officials were happy about it, but Kristine knew how to work the system. She was never charged with a disciplinary action; therefore, she shouldn't have to face any unnecessary changes. Since she was a model prisoner and had an excellent work ethic, she was quickly relocated to the REC building. Mr. Piquant was moved to outside yard detail, manning the incoming and outgoing vehicles with little or no contact with the women.

Life returned to normal however. Those 12 days that she spent in lockdown broke her a little more. She was trapped in a cell with no contact and having to beg to go to the bathroom. She couldn't do anything other than think, something that she didn't give herself the chance to do when she was in open population.

Just looking out the window made her feel the hardness of her conviction. She was in a concrete cell that offered no comfort. She was limited to items that she could order on commissary and there were no medications to treat her allergies, which were made worse by the summer air. She was forced to think about her losses and she cried until it physically hurt. To make matters worse, due to a miscommunication by officers, Kristine was denied a visit due to her being on lockdown. The matter was quickly resolved, but not before her mother had already left the prison. It made her angry and even if she knew that she had broken the rules, she also knew that they never had a case against her. She had covered all her bases. The time spent in lockdown was just another way that her wrongful conviction crushed her spirit. She didn't know if she would ever have a normal relationship again. Prison life had changed the way she viewed the world, especially relationships. She should have been able to explore normal relationships.

In 2001, Kristine graduated magna cum laude from Ball

State University with a Bachelor's degree in English. She was dressed, covered by a black robe, looking like any other college graduate, except for the fences and officials surrounding the event. She still had her head high as she knew that her accomplishment was huge. She was her grandfather's only grandchild to graduate college - a fact that she knew he was proud of and she was proud of as well.

She had another reason to be proud. I was receiving my Associate's degree. She was experiencing her own joy and my joy of graduation as well. It was a graduation that I wouldn't have achieved if she hadn't been there and pushed me to succeed. The ceremony was followed by a two -hour lunch for the inmates, a special catered event provided by the prison's cooking class. The event was a chance for the inmates to celebrate their achievement with loved ones and a chance for good food rarely eaten by the inmates. The air was full of happiness and laughter as the inmates enjoyed this moment with their family. It was a moment of celebration for Kristine, even if it was behind fences wrapped in barbed wire. She was proud that her son could be there to witness her accomplishment and even if he didn't fully understand at the age of 6, he was still there supporting his mommy.

Chapter Nine: Bringing Awareness to her Darkness

With every passing year that Kristine was imprisoned, she was living in a daily nightmare where every day her life was slipping away. The darkness wasn't just in the night, it lasted even when the sun was out. She was trapped in this nightmare of her unjust sentence and couldn't escape. The daily routine of the prison was part of her darkness. She was left to wonder at every moment how Trent was doing. She longed to have a different routine, one that centered on her growing son.

One of the biggest problems with inmates who are wrongly convicted in the judicial system is lack of resources. It is hard to believe in innocence when it seems that guilt is all over the news. Most wrongly convicted cases are handled by state public defenders, which depending on the county could be massively overworked and underfunded. State budgets determine how much money is allotted to the public defender's office. Over worked defense attorneys often opt for plea deals than a better defense. It is not uncommon that a county lawyer has more plea deals a year than trials ending in not guilty verdicts. As much as they believe in someone's innocence, there is lack of funding for a proper defense.

We live in a society where "innocent until proven guilty" doesn't exist. People are convicted by the media rather than waiting for the jury's ruling. The media can influence the potential jurors of a case, even if they don't admit to it. The influence that the media has on a case has only become more powerful with the era of social media. In some cases, there are Facebook pages that either support a person's innocence, or pages that call for the harsh punishments for the defendant. There is no balance between justice and truth. The justice that people demand for often outweighs the truth. The truth is forgotten as public's outcry for justice is demanded. With no balance, the defendant is left to defend their innocence and, in many cases, they start that upsetting journey alone.

Benjamin Franklin said, "it is better that 100 guilty persons should escape than that one innocent person should suffer."[6] His statement was made in 1785, at a time when America was in its infancy, trying to figure out how to build a successful government. The Constitution was the first attempt at establishing a stable judicial system to have a successful government. As a founder of America, Franklin was one of the seven men that would lay the groundwork for justice in America. Franklin's sentiments on justice leads to the belief that he wanted a government that respected the idea of justice.

Kristine was convicted before the era of social media, which today is helpful to bring awareness to cases. Social media was not as present then as it is today, which hurt Kristine's fight for justice. In the recent years, we have watched as the nation took to Twitter to voice their outrage over the 2015 Netflix's

---

[6] Benjamin Franklin, Works 293 (1970), Letter from Benjamin Franklin to Benjamin Vaughan (14 March 1785)

documentary "Making a Murderer." The ten-part series featured

Steven Avery and Brendon Dassey, who many believe are

wrongfully convicted of murder. A documentary that was written

and directed by Laura Ricciardi and Moira Demos and was 10

years in the making, "Making a Murderer" shows the flaws from

the beginning of the case against the duo. Since the release of the

documentary, people are more familiar with the case and

therefore are more supportive.

Kristine did not have any such support. She had her

family's support, but being inexperienced in the media world hurt

her chances of having her case reviewed by millions. She was

determined to keep fighting and look for any way to bring some

awareness to her darkness. That chance came in 2000, when

Mariah told her about Jennifer Furio. Furio was writing a book

that would center on letters from women prisoners. The concept

was something Furio had done before in a previous book.

In 2001, Furio, who wrote a book called "The Serial Killer

Letters: A Penetrating Look Inside the Minds of Murderers," was writing a new book "Letters from Prison: Voices of Women Murderers." Kristine's letters were featured in a chapter and new attention came from the book. Unlike the other women featured in the book, Kristine did not hold back on proclaiming her innocence. She was desperate to get home to her young son and raise him.

Kristine knew that she had to try everything to get her case heard and knew that the media could help her. She wrote letters to Jennifer Furio, which were later published in the book, along with other women that were incarnated for murders. Kristine wrote in one of the first letters "I'm desperate for help. I need someone to help me, even if it means becoming another television tabloid freak."[7]

She knew that her best hope for a new trial was to get the public involved. If people knew her struggle and all that she had gone through, they would realize that an innocent mother was

[7] Furio, J. (2001). *Letters from prison: voices of women murderers*. New York: Algora Pub.

being wrongly imprisoned. At the time of the publication of the book, she had been locked up for six years missing five birthdays with her young son, Trent.

Kristine was left to find a lawyer and ways to get her story told, while keeping up with her busy schedule. She spent more time looking for information. She had begun to change her thinking, no longer believing that the answers would find her. She started an eight-month program through Blackstone to get her paralegal certification. She also took a job in the law library to give her more exposure to the law books that were there for prisoners to view. She was going to find something that could help her and a future lawyer.

Kristine was starting to realize that they took her freedom, but they couldn't take her spirit. She started to rely on her faith more and her education to find a way to tell her truth. She knew her truth and she was determined to make others see it too. Her quest for justice was fueled by her pain and her anger. There wasn't a moment that she stopped believing in the truth, nor did she allow her anger to show. She wouldn't become bitter and the fight within herself, which was harder than she could express.

The decision to do the book was easy for her. It was a way that her story could be told. It was a way to get exposure to her dead case. She was beyond frustrated with the system and her lack of understanding made it impossible to see how to fight. The more she learned about the law, the more she loved it. She could even imagine becoming a lawyer after her release, whenever it came.

Furio added a few pages explaining the case, not necessarily to explain the prisoner's letters, but to help the readers picture the crime. With Kristine's case, Furio wrote "Other stories in this book involve confessions, denials, obvious instances of insanity, and that gray area where imprisonment comes as the result of another's actions. We can make some sense out of these cases. Yet, if ever there existed a story that could force the greatest skeptic to reconsider cynical views regarding a convicted person's plea of innocence, it would be the case of Kristine

Bunch."[8] However even with the author's tone set, when the book was published there wasn't any rush of help from potential lawyers as Kristine had secretly wished. There were a few letters from readers, which offered comfort but little else. Her life continued as inmate #966069 and the years were quickly mounting and inching close to a decade.

September 2001, brought another loss to Kristine's life. Tom Claxton died. The man that had been a second father to her was gone. As she listened to her mother tell her the news, her reality hit in a new way. There were some that wouldn't likely be alive when she was released. The pain of his death caused Kristine to fight a war within herself. She was so lost in her grief of Tony and now she had to sit there and accept Tom's death without closure. She was unable to attend his funeral and even if it had been her biological father, it was unlikely that the DOC would

---

[8] Furio, J. (2001). *Letters from prison: voices of women murderers*. New York: Algora Pub.

have approved her to go due to her lengthy sentence. She had to try to make sense of this loss alone. The nights of tears continued as she faced a reality of who else she could lose before her release in 2026.

Another interesting change happened around the time Kristine was writing Furio and learning about different innocence law clinics. She had spent all these years feeling like she was all alone in the system. She was starting to see more and more about wrongful convictions. By now, the outside world was connected by the internet, something that Kristine had no access to. Social media sites were starting up, mostly through email, such as Yahoo or AOL and different forms of journalism were happening. People were writing more comprehensive pieces that most local newspapers wouldn't write. That different writing became a reality for Americans, so did the way they would view justice.

Kristine started asking her family for more articles or anything that they could find to send her through the mail. She had a new connection to the outside world, due to my release in

2002. My release was hard, but also rewarding. She believed that she had raised this little girl into a woman who would soar out there. She even made sure that she told me this on the morning of my release. "Go soar, baby. I will be there soon." Through letters and phone calls, Kristine would relate the information that she needed. She didn't know exactly what she was looking for in those early days but she knew that she would find the needle in the haystack. Finding the needle was her only mission.

Chapter Ten: No Escape Plan for the Innocent

For Kristine Bunch, there was never an escape plan. She still believed that her innocence would set her free from her 60-year sentence. She believed that the truth always prevailed against injustice. She believed that if you are innocent, then you fight. Fighting was all that she had left. Her only plan of freedom was to find a dream team to help fight the system.

She knew that an escape plan was useless and would require her to be dishonest. Her values were something that she couldn't comprise. It was all she had left of the shell of the person that she had become. Her values were simple by most standards, but they grounded her. Her escape plan had to be a legal plan. The thought of always looking over her shoulder scared her more than the legal system. It was picking the lesser of two evils - one that could get her killed or one that could clear her name. She knew that the judicial system was set up to help the innocent and held onto that belief.

By 2002, Kristine had completed most of the trades that offered a time cut to her sentence and was working in the law library as a job and was still working with the late-night kitchen crew. She was having her annual picnics with her family and regular visits with Trent. She would leave the visitation room just as defeated as the first visit with Trent, feeling hopeless about getting out to raise him. She would listen to her family as they tried to fill in all the happy moments that Trent was experiencing. They wanted her to only hear the good. By doing this, even Trent learned how to shield things from his mother. Trent learned how to tell his mother things were good, but she would later find out they weren't. He didn't share details about his home life that would have likely caused Kristine more agony. He was getting to an age where his mother's conviction was beyond his understanding. He was just a boy and the only thing that he had to hold onto was his visits with his mom. He was fiercely loyal to his Nana - who by all rights had earned that loyalty. Kristine knew that she was just trying to do her best by Trent, but beliefs would fade as the reality of Trent's behaviors were brought to her attention. She believed that there were only minor infractions and typical young boy behaviors.

Kristine knew that she was losing Trent, but believed that if she made it out before his 18th birthday she could fix it. It was impossible to explain the bond that she felt with her son, even though she had never gotten the chance to raise him outside the prison. She could envision a life of the two visiting amusement parks or going fishing as she had when she was a child.

The depression never went away as she faced every morning to begin her daily routines. Three was never a time she couldn't feel the raw pain of her sentence. She was hanging onto every day by a thread and more threads unraveled daily. Probably to cope with the pain, she started to focus on how to help herself.

With each passing year, she focused on her release. It was freedom that engulfed her dreams. She couldn't wait to be there for Trent when he got off the bus from school or to plan one of his birthday parties. It was a dream that gave her the strength to fight. Her love for her son and knowing that she was innocent kept her from running. She knew that innocent people fought for their truth.

Working in the law library gave Kristine more access to law books and research that she did not have in her cell. As hard as she tried, she didn't understand the language of the fire reports. However, a fellow inmate, Kelly, * [9]who was serving time for fraud, offered some assistance. She told Kristine to reach out to her husband who was a fire chief. He could help her better understand the language. He helped her get on the right track about the ATF lab results and the fire analysis. She would research her case on her down-time and one case that got her attention was Willingham v. State of Texas.

In 1992, Cameron Todd Willingham was convicted of murdering his three young daughters when a fire destroyed the family home. Like Kristine's case, there was no motive found to be

---

[9] (name changed to protect identity)

able to support his arrest. From the beginning of the police investigation, they asserted that Willingham started the fire to cover up his abuse of the girls - a claim that his wife Stacy Kuykendall flatly denied to investigators. However, the fire investigators believed that they had found burn patterns and ruled it arson.

Willingham was executed by the State of Texas on February 17, 2004, after years of proclaiming his innocence. For years after his death, lawyers would try to get the State of Texas to reserve his conviction based on the findings. His conviction still stands on the Texas books, but enough reasonable doubt is there that if he was not executed, he would likely be freed today. There is no justice in killing an innocent man.

Like Kristine, Willingham was arrested because an arson was believed to be the cause of the fire. Arson investigators look for burn patterns, or evidence of accelerants used to start to the fire. They look for the cause of the fire and in some cases, it is junk science. Arson investigation has rapidly changed throughout the years, perhaps faster than fire investigators can keep up.

With each new case that is studied by investigators who are experts in this field, new theories can be determined that can help understand the patterns of fire. Old methods that many arson investigators still believe are ways that can determine if a fire is arson or not are now outdated and unreliable. The old belief was that if there are burn patterns that means an arson is the only logical conclusion. This has been proven wrong and is junk science.

Kristine knew that a PCR (Post Conviction Relief) was her best option for gaining freedom, however she also knew that she needed a lawyer. She knew that she didn't understand the law enough to file this motion. It was painful for her to watch her son grow up outside the fences knowing that she was innocent. The stigma that her conviction placed on Trent also was devastating to her. She knew that her son was struggling in school and being on ADHD medications did not help, a choice that she never supported. She was watching her son fade into the background and she needed to get to him.

Chapter Eleven: Building a Dream Team

For years, Kristine Bunch never lost hope that someone would take her case. She wrote hundreds of letters over the years, most came back with the standard "sorry but we can't take your case," or asking for huge sums of money to take her case. Kristine read the letters and wondered how she could ever afford $25,000 just for the lawyer to take her case. She was lucky to make $30 dollars a month with her state pay. She wrote numerous innocence projects asking for their assistance. One of those was the Northwestern University Bluhm Legal Clinic, who wrote her back saying that they did not have the resources or staff to take on her case. There was little hope that she would be helped and her sentence was feeling more crushing with each day as Trent was getting older. Kristine had to get fighting even though her fight seemed hopeless.

In 2003, Kristine wrote another letter to a lawyer after another inmate told her about a great lawyer that she knew. She wrote Hilary Bowe-Ricks and to her happiness Hilary didn't send her the standard letter, instead she came to her with true hope. Hilary also offered Kristine something that no one else had before - her belief in her innocence. All Hilary had to start her case with was Kristine's letter and an article that she had found on new science of fire investigators. Hilary had just given her real hope by believing in her. After eight years, she finally had hope that the truth would be spoken. Kristine had her family and friends believed in her, but here was this person who believed in her and didn't have to. She finally felt that she wasn't alone. Someone believed in her innocence and knowing that it was an uphill battle, Hilary was willing to fight it with Kristine. From the moment Kristine met Hilary, she knew that she had finally found the missing link to her fight. Hilary offered to take Kristine's case and was willing to accept her monthly state pay as payments.

With little to go on, Hilary looked at other cases that could help Kristine's case. Hilary found an article written by John Lentini, a leading expert in fire science. Since 1975, John Lentini has been testifying in courts as an expert on arson and different fires. He also was a pioneer in the discoveries in junk science and through his experiences and research believed that some methods used by fire investigators was outdated. He has shown that fires that were ruled arson were accidentally set. He wrote an article called "The Lime Street Fire: Another Perspective," where he had been a witness for the prosecution and was ready to testify in a few days. However, with the prosecutor's office, wanting a clear and detailed statement, Lentini did an experiment along with the defense and prosecutors watching, he had not proven that the suspect was innocent but that it was possible. This finding led him to research other fires and the methods used to determine the cause. He would later be quoted as saying ""If you survive a fatal fire, you've got a very good chance of being charged with setting it."[10]

---

[10] Berman, T. (2010, May 05). Top Five Arson Fire Myths. Retrieved March 16, 2017, from http://abcnews.go.com/2020/fire-arson-mythsmisunderstandings/story?id=10540364

Finding this article gave Kristine a hope that she didn't have before; a possible link to her own case. She got copies of the article so she could include that along with her letters of pleas to lawyers. She began to get as much information to help support her theory that the arson report was wrong, she just didn't know how to prove it yet.

By 2006, Hilary Ricks was still working hard on Kristine's defense and while Kristine could not be working alongside her lawyer, she could aid in her defense. Kristine had gotten her paralegal certification in 2005 and was working in the prison law library helping other inmates with their legal needs.

Hilary filed a petition of post-conviction relief with Kristine's county under the same judge in 2006. A post-conviction relief is a legal proceeding that challenges the conviction and the validity of the case. The first wheel to Kristine's freedom was spinning. She knew that the petition could take years and still her conviction might not be overturned, however, she also knew that she had to fight. Now 11 years into her 60-year sentence, Trent was 11 years old and she needed to be there to finish raising him. She needed more than a few hours a month and the dream of holding him while he slept was making her stand strong. For all these years, the losses mounted, the heartaches continued, and the nightmare never ended, but she was becoming the phoenix and was rising from the ashes. She was fighting for the truth and her truth would set her free.

Hilary knew that she needed more help on the case, she needed experts and more resources. With Kristine's case being based on science, there was more evidence that needed to be properly investigated. She would file motions to delay so she could find those resources, or a clear smoking gun.

Per Kristine's request, Hilary Bowe-Ricks reached out to the fire investigators that were discussed in the arson myth article and to their surprise, Richard Roby offered help that included 10 hours pro-bono to the defense team and the assistance of Jamie McAllister, a young staffer in his office. It was an offer of help that Kristine had long needed and while it offered hope, Kristine wasn't holding her breath before celebrating.

Over the years, prison volunteers would be intrigued by Kristine's strength. The way she remained graceful and determined even after years of being wrongly convicted. She was a friend to many and offered compassion to those in need. She didn't have many enemies within the fences, as she treated others with respect. Even among the prison guards, she was respected. Kristine was not bitter towards others and her personality was positive throughout her time. One of the volunteers from Kairos, Betsy Marks, especially believed in her innocence. Kristine met Betsy through Kairos, a large Christian organization that connects people from the outside with the inside.

Betsy believing in Kristine's innocence, wrote many letters to the Northwestern University Center for Wrongful Convictions, Bluhm Legal clinic asking that Jane Raley be given the opportunity to look over Kristine's case. She even called daily to ensure that Kristine's voice could be heard.

The Bluhm Legal Clinic opened their doors with two attorneys, but the concept can be dated back to 1910 when John Henry Wigmore started the idea. The law clinic uses students in aid for their cases and they can take on more cases. One of the first cases that is listed on their website is the case of Tabitha Pollock. Her 3-year-old daughter was killed by her live-in boyfriend and the prosecution contended that she should have known how dangerous her boyfriend was. She was sentenced to 36 years in prison. She served seven years before lawyer Jane Raley could bring her home.

The Bluhm Legal clinic consider Kristine's case with the help of experts and looked at her background and mental health and they found nothing to raise concern. Kristine was a good client to represent for the clinic and they believed in her case even before they officially met Kristine.

Jane Raley later stated that she was having a hard time not telling Kristine at that first visit that they would be taking on her case. "Here we had a woman with no prior criminal history. No eyewitness. No confession. No motive. And the experts we were consulting with were telling us that there was no scientific basis to suggest arson. We had a perfect case."[11] Jane didn't tell Kristine that she believed in her but Kristine felt hope after that visit. Something that made her sleep a little easier that night, there was hope.

After having met with Kristine officially in 2007, the clinic took on Kristine's case. After Jane Raley looked at the case, she spoke to her fire experts and they all agreed that Kristine could be innocent. Jane Raley and the Bluhm Legal Clinic joined Kristine's dream team. Bowe-Ricks stayed on pro bono and worked as a liaison with the Northwestern law clinic. The lawyers started digging into the case.

The more that Kristine's team of lawyers dug into the evidence, the more the Decatur County prosecutors resisted their efforts. They would be missing key pieces of evidence - evidence

[11] Fernandez, M. (2015, December 23). When Will Kristine Bunch Be Free? Retrieved January 26, 2017, from http://www.indianapolismonthly.com/longform/when-will-kristine-bunch-befree/

that would ultimately show that there was no arson, just an electric fire. Finding the missing evidence would lead to more questions for Kristine. Questions that may never be answered for her, only haunt her for years to come.

Kristine filed a Freedom of Information Act, but no new information was given to her. Her lawyers then filed a petition for discovery and found something that would change the case. To their surprise, they were given the original report that was still in her file with the Washington D.C. office. In that report, Forensic Chemist William Kinard stated that there was no arson. The report that introduced to the jurors in Kristine's trial was altered from this report. It is unclear why that report was altered or who altered the report.

Kristine wondered why the report was altered or who made the decision to frame an innocent grieving mother. She was forced to ponder how they could sleep at night while she was forced to sleep on a metal bed with a two-inch cot that was her mattress. She laid there at night trying to understand the reason that someone wanted to take away her freedom. For Kristine, if she allowed herself to think about why they altered the report, her pain was greater. It was the most crushing thing that she had felt so far in her ordeal. That altered report took everything from her, her dreams, her hopes, and every moment with her son Trent. Whoever altered the report took everything. It is unclear who altered the report, it could have been William Kinard, or the fire investigators who from the beginning of their investigation felt it was arson. She was lost in a legal system without a reason. The reason behind why the report was altered is almost as important as the years that Kristine went through a mind-crushing loss that had left her feeling broken and like a shattered vase that could never be restored to its original glory. It was that decision of altering the ATF report that changed Kristine's fate.

The reason that Kinard altered the report was important, however, it could not bring any type of justice for Kristine - maybe some closure for her injustice. The fact that the report was altered was unknown to Kristine for over 10 years. The finding of the altered report did not bring Kristine any relief, instead it furthered her fuel for her fight. Her fight was more important than ever. She had to prove the whole case against her was an injustice caused by one person, Willard Kinard, a forensic chemist employed by the ATF. He was the reason that the Decatur County Prosecutor's Office also believed that this young mother was guilty of setting fire to her trailer. His handwritten notes changed this fire to arson.

Finding this unaltered report did not bring closure, nor did it bring justice for Kristine. The report proved that there was no reason for the trial. It also showed that someone with power altered Kristine's life forever. There will never be justice for that kind of malicious behavior. Finding the original, unaltered report brought more questions for her. Now instead of asking herself who could hate her so much that they would set her trailer on fire, now she was asking why the investigators framed her. How did they determine that the fire was not anything but accidental fire? She had to wonder why she had been framed. Is it the common belief that if someone survives a fire and others do not, that the survivor must have done it? Finding the unaltered report was another loss that Kristine had to face. She had to learn to deal with her anger over the already lost years.

Another thing that the lawyers wanted to uncover was the missing data of the lie detector that Kristine had supposedly failed. It was not used in the trial as lie detectors are not used in court. However, the data could be useful to the defense and could possibly help the lawyers see why the investigation centered on her from the beginning. The missing data could have accidentally been lost or deliberately lost to help the prosecutor's case. Since the lie detector results were never located; Kristine's new defense team could not have them analyzed. It remains a mystery as to whether or not Kristine really failed the test as the detectives claimed to the previous leak to the media back in 1996, the day before her trial. It was another question for Kristine and made her wonder if being framed started the moment she survived the fire.

Since no tests were given to Kristine on the night of the

fire, there is no test results showing how much carbon monoxide had poisoned her during the fire. There is no data to know how much she was affected by the smoke. The effects of carbon monoxide poisoning can be headaches, weakness, blurred vision and even confusion. In her confusion, she could have easily thought that she heard Tony's voice after awaking to the smoke that June morning. Maybe the real miracle is that she did hear his voice. That hallucination could have saved her a certain death. This missing test could have shown how she was a victim of the fire too, not the predator.

It was another loss that added to Kristine's long list. She now had to deal with the emotions of knowing that the report that signed her arrest warrant was a lie. It made her have more doubts and even more questions. It added an enormous amount of pain to her already huge mountain of grief. A grief that had no ending.

As her lawyers fought for her freedom, Kristine was left to deal with the changes of the prison. Street clothes were taken away for the standard prison uniforms. Kristine's new wardrobe consisted of white undergarments, beige uniforms, and grey sweatshirts that could only be worn under the uniforms. Along with the uniforms, many of the privileges that Blank had allowed over the years were taken away. Annual picnics and even the summer camp that was offered for the mothers and children were reduced to one day. Visitation hours were changing, reducing the amount of time that prisoners could see their families. Kristine was left to wonder how much more she could lose before the lawyers saved her.

There were moments of despair where she wondered if she would survive. She hadn't had a good health checkup in years and the cost outweighed the low quality of the checkup. She was worried that she would die before the courts would see her injustice and set her free. The amount of stress that was upon the prison was affecting all including the officers who seem to be projecting their troubles on inmates. She recalled the years after Blank's retirement as the hardest. There wasn't anyone left to care for the prisoners. It had become the one thing that Blank never would have wanted - inhumane.

Even when with the Bluhm Legal clinic, including Jane Raley and Karen Daniels on the legal team, they needed more assistance on the case and reached out to Ron Shafer in 2008.

Ron Shafer's experience was impressive to say the least. He had nine years' experience working as a lead prosecutor and a year working in the Chicago's U.S. Attorney's Office as chief of the criminal division and then returning to private practice soon after.

When Ron Shafer first met Kristine, he asked her if he could defend her. He told her that he had prosecuted many arson cases and her case wasn't arson. Kristine was left speechless. Here was this successful attorney who believed in her innocence and was asking for her permission to take on her case? She was humbled and from that moment she knew that she loved him. She wasn't used to this type of contact from the world and didn't know that people like him existed. The mere fact that he asked her to fight her case was amazing to her. As he shared his experience, with his success rates as a federal prosecutor, she listened with a new hope. People like him did exist. She had long given up on mankind. Kristine happily accepted his offer of help and Ron Safer brought Kelly Warner, another lawyer in his firm, to add to the "dream team."

Chapter Twelve: The Final Fight begins

Wrongfully convicted has become part of the American justice system. It is a term that lawyers are saying more and more over the last decade. The process of proving oneself from guilty to innocent can take years to unravel and politics has overtaken the minds of jurors. Yet, jury members are becoming smarter, in part because of new television shows that show just how easy it is to be wrongfully convicted. Juries are learning how to better read the evidence or the lack of evidence in trials.

Although the term is new, it has been around for over a century. The first documented wrongful murder conviction in the United States is thought to be Jesse Boorn and Stephen Boorn. In 1812, Russell Colvin disappeared from Manchester, Vermont, and for seven years, the town speculated that his brothers-in-law, Jesse and Stephen Boorn killed him for unknown reasons. Both brothers, under pressure, confessed to killing him, which they both recanted later. Even though the bones that were found earlier were believed to be human bones, they were later revealed to be of animal origins, a jury still convicted the Boorn brothers and they were sentenced to death. However, Russell Colvin suddenly reappeared months before, just in time to save the Boorn brothers from execution.

The defenders of the legal system, the hard-working defense lawyers, have everything to gain if their client is found not guilty, whereas the prosecutor, police, and investigators have nothing to lose, even if they lie. In Indiana, there is no punishment for those who lie to suspects just to gain a conviction. Police detectives can lie to the accused and even intimidate the suspect without fear of prosecution. As in Kristine's case, they can even falsify a report to indicate a crime happened, even if it never happened.

The ultimate nightmare is that anyone can be falsely accused of any crime. The judicial system isn't setup to help prevent the innocent from being wrongly convicted. However, there are different ways that the innocent are convicted. Whether it is a false confession, or planted evidence by police officials. Just watch any detective on those true crime shows, when they believe that they have a suspect that was good for the crime, they will not stop until they gain a conviction. There are different cases that show how far detectives will go to get a conviction against an innocent person. There are many different techniques that law enforcement uses to interrogate suspects.

In the documentary "Scenes of a Crime," viewers got a first-hand look at the police interrogation of Adrian Thomas. The documentary, directed by Blue Hadaegh and produced by Grover Babcock, showed New York detectives questioning Thomas for 10 hours. During the 10 hours, you could see the different techniques, including intense psychological manipulation that led to Thomas's false confession. You hear his claims of innocence from the beginning and how the police convinced him that he had thrown his infant son accidently. Their reports of evidence were lies that the detectives told Thomas and gave him different scenarios of accidents that could have happened. To the surprise of Thomas after he gave the detectives a "confession," he was arrested and quickly claimed his innocence. This documentary showed how police treated this scared young father and how they abused their power by lying to get a confession that was built on lies from Thomas and even the detectives. It clearly shows how justice was tainted by police detectives looking for an easy confession.

In recent years, more videos of police interrogations have surfaced including the interrogation of Branden Dassey. In "Making a Murderer," you can clearly see how a scared young boy confessed to a crime that he had no knowledge of. You can hear as they feed him details that only a murderer would know, or that a detective could suspect. There is no line for law enforcement - they may act like the villain or savior for the suspect - in some cases getting a false confession, which makes it even harder for the suspect to recant. Even if a confession is forced, the police do not admit any wrongdoing, nor is there any fear of prosecution. People have a hard time believing the suspect is innocent when they confess. To simply say "I only confessed because I was scared," is hard to imagine for most people. No one believes that anyone would confess to something that they didn't do. Most people wonder how someone could say that they did something that they didn't. Even when the evidence doesn't line up with the "confession," they are still willing to believe the words. Potential jurors may only hear the confession of the suspect, since most suspects don't testify in court in fear of hurting their case. It is another way that the innocent is silenced by one-sided investigations.

With police interrogations rapidly getting worse, more confessions are being questioned in the social media. The message that there are innocent people locked up is being spread across the world and especially in social media. It is getting easier to see how false confessions are happening. The police have all the control over the suspect, many never having any contact with police before. People are unprepared for the different methods that the detectives are trained with. When they go into that interrogation room, they are not prepared for the tactics that police will go to obtain a warrant. They have no idea that you should always ask for a lawyer, even you are innocent.

In the case of The State of Wisconsin vs. Steven Avery, there is clear evidence that the Manitowoc County Sheriff's Department knew that another suspect confessed to the sexual assault against the victim. Sheriff Thomas Kocurek told the Brown County police detective not to worry about it and that they were sure, that they had the right suspect. Avery spent 18 years in prison before DNA cleared him of the sexual assault charges. There were also reports that the sheriff's department's forensic artist purposely drew a picture of Avery for the victim, which could have been the reason that she chose Avery in a photo lineup that was shown to her after the attack. It is possible to conclude that the sheriff's department framed Avery for the crime. Avery later settled his lawsuit against Manitowoc County for $400,000 in February 2006.

However, there are cases like Kristine Bunch where no

crime was committed. In the case of Jennifer Del Prete, a daycare worker who served 10 years for the death of a 3-month infant that was in her care for degree murder, she was accused of shaking the baby, which resulted in Shaken Baby Syndrome. Shaken Baby Syndrome cases have become increasingly questioned over the last few years. The science is questionable and more experts that once supported it are now saying that the science is wrong.

Neuropathologist Dr. Waney Squier wrote a report that stated a 4-month-old baby was a victim of shaken baby syndrome, however when the mother appealed her conviction, Dr. Squier's opinion changed and she was an expert for the defense. Her opinion changed due to the new discoveries in science, many that she had done herself. She was quoted as saying "Over the past ten years so much more has been discovered about how a baby's brain develops in its first year and these developments have seriously undermined SBS,"[12] she explains. The discoveries have

[12] MailOnline, A. L. (2011). Retrieved from http://www.dailymail.co.uk/femail/article-1382290/At-half-parentstried-shaken-baby-syndrome-wrongly-convicted-expert-warns.html

helped defense lawyers to get a better defense for their clients.

Throughout the years, Kristine had not attended the weddings of her family or friends who got married. It didn't bother her as much as it did when her brother, Michael got married. Michael married his longtime girlfriend on a winter day in January 2009. She was happy for her brother and wanted to be there, instead of her cold steel bed in the middle of 39 women with their own issues. She knew that her case was moving in the right direction, but how many more moments would she be forced to miss. She had two nieces whose births she couldn't be there for and now she missed her little brother's wedding - a huge blow to her heart. Whatever she had left in her to fight with was fading with each new loss, losses seemed to outweigh the gains in her life.

The anger that Kristine felt by this point was heartbreaking to those who knew about her state of mind. They knew that she was fighting a daily battle not to give up, even though it would have been so much easier to stop. If she would have stopped, she would have to accept her fate. Fighting meant that she had to keep her head up and smile through the pain. Others would point out her strength to her and she would nod her head saying "Thanks." However, inside she was angry. The last 13 years she had been stripped down to her bones and carried the weight of this atrocious sentence for her child. There are no words that could ever describe the anger that she felt and the light at the end of the tunnel seemed out of grasp. She was unable to feel normal joy due to the anger, but she wore that smile that everyone expected to see. They couldn't see the pain and anger behind a smile that could blossom a rose in the middle of winter. The cross that she was carrying was cutting her from the inside out. It was simply too hard to keep fighting, yet her innocence wouldn't allow her to stop. It was a double-edged sword, either way she would have to face an inconceivable agony.

Chapter Thirteen: A Deal Exchange for Innocence

Kristine has always maintained that the justice system isn't broken, it is just that the people running it are broken and clouded by their own views. She still believed in the judicial system and that the same system that wrongly convicted her would fix their error. There is a reason that there is a process to the untangling wrongful convictions, a reason that doesn't benefit the accused. The process of untangling injustice can take years, even when DNA doesn't match the suspect. No prosecutor wants to admit that their investigation or their conviction was tainted. The more convincing the issues are to overturn, the more seldom prosecutors admit flaws in their cases. There is a lack of remorse, no public apology and only their own defense against wrongdoing. It is sad that the same people telling the world that the suspect has no remorse shows no remorse when the evidence clearly shows an innocent person has just lost years of their lives.

The summer of 2009 brought a deal from the Decatur

County prosecutor's office - a deal that would require Kristine to plead guilty and then she would be released in six more years. Even as Jane Raley was telling Kristine the deal, she was wondering what the right choice was to make. If she pled guilty, then she would forever be labeled a murderer. She would be admitting that she was responsible for the death of Tony. In return she would have an outdate that was close and more imaginable than 2020. Her son would only be 20 in six years.

Kristine sat there listening to her lawyer telling her that her freedom could be closer than she had ever imagined. She could plead guilty and go home when Trent was 20, or she could keep fighting with and go home when he was 26. As a lawyer, Jane Raley was under obligation to take the prosecutor's deal to Kristine. Kristine was left to question whether her team believed in her anymore. She didn't fully understand that Jane was acting under the ethics that she swore upon when taking her oaths as a lawyer. She wondered if they did not see the war as winnable and if this battle's victory was at least a sooner outdate. She asked

Jane over and over "What should I do?" She wanted her freedom so badly and this was at least an outdate that she could count down to. She wanted out more than anything else in the world and she wanted to be there with her son. She wanted to be there with her family and experience their moments. She wanted to be freed. She had already missed the first 13 years of her son's life. Her little boy was rapidly growing into a man and she wanted to be there to take him all the places that she couldn't.

As her family and Trent would tell Kristine of all the adventures that he had, it saddened her because she wanted to do all of those things with him first. She needed to be there when he conquered all his newfound adventures of life. She was missing every moment that he was experiencing and she was missing out on being able to live those moments with him. She wanted the chance to see him graduate high school or go off to college. The years were not on her side as her sentence carried into 13-years of stolen time.

The decision was not easy. She still believed that her

innocence was worth fighting for. She made Trent a promise that she would come home to him before he turned 18 and she also was trying to raise him with values. She had to continue to fight. She was innocent and she would not lie to gain her freedom. The value of her freedom was worth more than lies and she was determined that her freedom would come by the truth - her truth of innocence. She turned the offer down knowing that she could be turning down her last chance of an early release. She had to stand up for her truth. She did not set the fire that killed her son.

Kristine didn't make the decision to not take the deal lightly. She made the decision based on the values that she wanted Trent to live by. All she had to give him was her truth and she would be lying if she took the deal. She couldn't admit to something that she did not do. She couldn't admit to a crime that she knew in her heart that she was innocent of committing. She wasn't going to show her son that you can lie to get what you wanted. No matter how badly she wanted to be out to be with Trent, she wasn't going to lie to get her release.

However, Kristine could not question her decision to turn down the deal and she had to put the armor back on. She would have to fight for the truth that she knew so well... she was innocent of setting her trailer on fire. She had to continue to live as DOC #966096 and focus on the things that she could control. Her daily behavior was not because she had accepted her fate, just another thing that she had to do to survive. Her status did not make her feel happiness, nor did the plea deal mean that she was going to be freed.

Kristine had told me after that plea that she was scared that she had just lost her last chance at freedom. As much as I reassured her that her day of truth was coming, she was the one stuck behind the walls of uncertainty. The prison had long changed leadership and where Ms. Blank had tried to make the prison as humane as possible, the new superintendent did not share the same beliefs.

Under the new superintendent, the prison conditions dramatically change. The inmates were charged per load of laundry and costs were increasing in every area. In the meantime, prison officials were cutting costs, such as on the food that was being served in the kitchen. Conditions within the dorms changed too and many nights the inmates were either too cold or too hot. Kristine recalled a hot summer when a huge fan that was aimed to cool inmates' dorms down in the blistering heat was broken and there was no urgency to fix it by officials. The inmates were trying to sleep in a sauna with full clothes on. There was no more of the communication that Blank had with inmates. The new warden was not there to have contact with the inmates. There was desperation in the air and more than the heat, it was crushing Kristine further into depression. She was just another inmate trying to survive and now she was hot as well.

November of 2009 brought a change of address for Kristine. The Indiana Women's Prison was being moved from downtown Indianapolis, 20 miles to the Girls' School. Prison officials made the move of 449 inmates in one day. The transfer was done by dorms and inmates were transferred to the new prison fully shackled. The new layout meant that Kristine would have a more private room as the new prison had a different layout. Each dorm had only a bunk set for two women. The move put the inmates on lock down for two weeks as the prison officials tried to maintain control in the new prison. The move was not an exciting move for Kristine. It wasn't the move that she wanted to make, home was the move she needed to make. The new prison would add more prisoners to the tight community that she was accustomed to and would change the way that she had known how to survive. The new prison also added 20 more minutes between her and her son. It added more stress on her already stressed out family.

There was, however, something that helped Kristine deal with the prison move. Her dream team got her an evidentiary hearing in November. Her PCR was working its way into through the judicial system and although she was not feeling that her odds were better, it was a start. The reason that she was frustrated was because the hearing would be in front of her original judge, John

Westhafer. She was transferred back to the Decatur County Courthouse for the hearing and her emotions were running high. She was happy that she was finally getting a chance to tell her truth. She was also faced with all the old emotions of this courtroom where she heard the word, "guilty" and had to listen to the same judge tell her that she would never raise her son years ago. It was a painful process for Kristine, however she knew the truth and she was there along her lawyers to fight for the truth.

Kristine's lawyers came prepared and were ready to defend her against the state. She felt taller sitting there along her lawyers, knowing that they believed in her innocence too, which was everything to Kristine. She knew that she had a fighting chance.13 years ago she wasn't confident in her defense but now she was. The lawyers were prepared with evidence that, once considered evidence against Kristine, now was evidence of innocence. The same evidence that was used to gain that guilty verdict was now going to be used to get her sentence overturned.

To strengthen their case, they brought experts to explain the new science of fire discovery.

Getting to this point was not an easy. There are requirements that must be met before new evidence can be introduced to be considered new evidence. "The nine requirements are (1) the evidence has been discovered since the trial; (2) it is material and relevant; (3) it is not cumulative; (4) it is not merely impeaching; (5) it is not privileged or incompetent; (6) due diligence was used to discover it in time for trial; (7) the evidence is worthy of credit; (8) it can be produced upon a retrial of the case; and (9) it will probably produce a different result at retrial."[13]

The defense knew that they were using the same evidence, however with a new and clear way to present the evidence as it should have been in her original trial. They also were alleging a Brady violation against the prosecution and ineffective counsel due to the evidence that would be presented.

---

[13] Retrieved January 10, 2017, from http://www.in.gov/judiciary/opinions/pdf/03211201mgr.pdf

The evidence was new because of the advancements in fire and toxicology science. Kristine's team also stated that they could disprove each piece of evidence that the Indiana Supreme Court used to uphold her conviction back in 1998. It was a mighty fight that all the lawyers and Kristine were ready to start.

The strongest expert was Jamie McAllister, whose credentials were impressive. She had Bachelor's and Master's degrees in Fire Protection Engineering and over 14 years' experience in fire investigation, including having investigated 200-300 fires to date. She was also pursuing a Ph.D. in Toxicology.

McAllister had studied all the eye witness testimony, examined the photos of the damaged trailer and Tony's toxicology report. She believed that the fire had started in a concealed place of the south bedroom of the trailer where Tony was sleeping that night. She also believed that it would have started in the space between the ceiling and the roof. It was only after burning through the ceiling tiles that the fire had dropped to the floor causing the flames to spread.

McAllister also said that based on Tony's level of carbon monoxide saturation being at 80% (which is fatal to a person at 50%) that he would have been consuming the carbon monoxide for at least 90 minutes. If he would have died in the fire -which undisputedly lasted only 30 minutes - he would have died by the flames of the fire. However, there was not any indication of burns to his lungs or to his trachea, something that she believed would have been present if he had been in the area where the fire was started as the state alleged. She said that a fire that is produced in a closed space creates more carbon monoxide than flames in an open space. She also said that the state's theory that there were two separate fires was impossible.

McAllister stated that Kristine's minor injuries were not consistent with someone who set the fire with a liquid accelerant. Her injuries were explained by the carbon monoxide levels in her system, which could have affected her senses and judgment. She also pointed to the medical records that indicated that Kristine had soot in her lungs, which was caused by the smoke that she had inhaled. Overall, her complete findings were that the fire had started accidentally in the closed space in the south bedroom.

Safer told Judge Westhafer that the advances in fire techniques had changed over the years since Kristine's first trial back in 1996. He referred the judge to the NFPA 921, a fire manual for fire investigators.

NFPA 921 is a guide for fire and explosion investigation, which is a peer reviewed document that is published by the National Fire Protection Association. It is regularly updated as new investigators disprove how fires are set or started. He also stated that the original findings of arson were not correct based on the updated journal and this meant that it was new evidence. He believed that a new jury would be able to find Kristine not guilty with the new experts that he brought with him.

Two of the experts were John Malooly, a former ATF agent and John DeHaun, an author who had written textbooks for fire investigations. Both agreed with the original report that no HPDs were found in the samples. Both experts were widely known to the prosecution, but it was rare to see them on the opposite side. No one disputed that kerosene could have been found since a source of heat for the trailer was a kerosene heater. When filling the heater, there were times that kerosene had been spilled as Kristine's mother, Susan, had explained during the original trial. However, the other samples that the state proved had HPDs were simply untrue. In an affidavit John Lentini, a world-renowned fire investigator, also gave his support for Kristine's defense.

The Brady violation occurred when ATF forensic chemist William Kinard took the stand in Kristine's first trial and spoke about the report that had been submitted to the defense in the discovery. Having found the un-altered original draft of Kinard's first report meant that he had lied on stand. Since his testimony was based on the final report, not the original report that he had submitted, which was not given to the defense. That original report should have been available to the defense at trial. Kristine's lawyer Frank Hamilton could use the inconsistencies in the two reports in preparing a better defense. The fact that it was concealed was a Brady violation against the state.

The lawyers argued that if the defense would have had the original report they could have questioned Kinard on his first findings and may have been able to raise reasonable doubt for the jurors. The altered report raised more questions than could be answered that morning, as the key players for the prosecution's case were absent. The state contented that the altered report had no bearing on their case, claiming instead it was just a piece of the case. Smith stood by his original trial, saying that the reports were available to the defense and that the original had no bearing on Kinard's testimony.

The moment that Kristine remembers as the best is the moment that Ron Shafer presented a photo of the "obstacle" that the state had claimed blocked the path of the bedroom door. As Ron Shafer showed the enlarged picture, William Smith, the Decatur County prosecutor, immediately objected to the picture and questioned the validity of the picture. Safer advised that the photo was in the photos given to him by the state, it was found in the evidence.

The discovery of the photo allowed the lawyers to show how the chair was not an obstacle to Tony's door. Kristine remembers feeling some victory, but what victory could she really feel as she looked at the picture. Her lawyers had just proved that there was nothing in the doorway, but she was no closer to understanding why her son died that fateful morning.

The state, even faced with all this new evidence, stood behind their conviction. Both the state and Kristine's dream team left that courtroom not knowing how the Judge would rule. They just had to wait for his ruling, which could take weeks or months. Kristine was returned to the prison feeling hopeful but cautious of the possibilities. She knew that she was only at the bottom of this mountain. She stood her ground and kept fighting.

On May 7, 2010, a typical Friday night for most Americans, but Kristine was in the dayroom of her dorm waiting for the investigation show "20/20" to come on. Her case was featured on the show along with two other cases: Amanda Kelley and Curtis Serverns. In all three cases, there was scientific evidence to refute that arson was the cause of the fires. For Kristine, she still believed in the judicial system, however that patience in a failing system was heartbreaking. She was fighting for the truth but it was painfully clear that others were also on that long road to justice. In the program, Jane Raley said "It's always difficult to unravel a wrongful conviction."[14]

After waiting for eight months, June 8, 2010, brought another blow to her case. Judge Westhafer denied Kristine's motion for her PCR (Post Conviction Relief). In his ruling, Westhafer said that there was no new evidence that could be presented to new jurors that would change the outcome of another trial. He also pointed to the fact that none of Kristine's new experts could say what the cause of the fire was. It was a

[14] Schadler, J., & Berman, T. (2010, May 05). Mom Served 14 Years for Arson Now Called 'Impossible' Retrieved January 07, 2017, from http://abcnews.go.com/2020/arson-investigation-evidencescience/story?id=10550837

crushing blow for Kristine, now 15 years into a 60-year sentence. Her son was now 14 years old and she knew that time was running out.

Kristine's dream team didn't waiver though and they immediately filed an appeal with the Indiana Court of Appeals. They prepared Kristine for a long wait as her case worked through the system and for all the possible outcomes including dismissing the case. If that were to happen, they would appeal to the Supreme Court. The months went by without word from the courts. She missed many important events in the lives of her family and with the wait- it was more painful.

Chapter Fourteen: Argument for Justice

On July 13, 2011, Ron Safer argued Kristine's case in front of a three-member panel of the Indiana Court of Appeals. It was a huge win for Kristine and her team of lawyers, as it is rare that cases get argued in front of a panel. Kristine could not watch as her team was fighting for her. In those 90 minutes, I watched as Ron Safer addressed the three judges. It was nothing like a movie, it was better. The amount of passion that Ron Safer spoke with for justice was nothing short of love and profound determination.

Every war has a pivotal battle that could be the turning point of the war; a battle that changed the course of the war. In the Civil War, the Battle of Gettysburg was the pivotal battle and had the highest casualties of the war. Over 50,000 American soldiers died during the three-day battle. It wasn't the end of the war, just the moment that the Confederates lost. It would take another two years before they would succeed to the Union. The battle of Gettysburg would change how each side would move forward.

For Kristine, the battle that would help with winning her war for her freedom was the hearing in July. The way that Ron Safer argued Kristine's case in front of those three judges was like a general leading his troops into unknown territory. He could show the injustice that Kristine had suffered for the last 15 years and continued to suffer daily. The truth was finally being exposed and the injustice was finally revealed.

Finally, months after the hearing on March 12, 2012, Hilary Bowe Ricks called Kristine via the counselor's phone to tell her the Indiana Court of Appeals ordered that her conviction be vacated. It was a real win for Kristine and for her team of lawyers. Hilary did warn Kristine that the state would probably appeal to the Supreme Court but it was a good thing for Kristine.

Kristine dreamed of gaining her freedom and attending law school to obtain her law degree with the hope of helping other prisoners who were wrongly convicted. She wanted to get released and make a difference for others. She felt that something had to come out of her situation that would help others. She studied for the LSAT using a book that someone had sent her. She started looking at life on the outside and what it would mean. She was trying to focus her mind on what was needed to achieve all of her dreams when she was released.

Kristine knew that her priority would be to get acquainted with Trent outside of the family preservation center and visits. She looked forward to watching him sleep, having dinner with him and discuss his day. She thought that Trent and she could move to a little apartment around the university where she would choose to go to law school. She knew that it would have its challenges, but couldn't she do it if she could survive this nightmare?

Kristine knew that the state would probably appeal. After all they had protested her PCR from the beginning. She was trying to prepare herself for that news. The balance between joy and the anxiety over waiting to see if the prosecutor was going to appeal the decision was overwhelming. She couldn't even feel the joy of having won a battle due to the swift attack by filing an appeal to the Supreme Court. She was dreaming of a future with her son while waiting for another battle. She was exhausted and every part of her was broken. She feared losing even though she knew that she was innocent. Her soul was lost and the thought of another long wait was terrifying. She was trying to be positive as her supporters were encouraging, but it was hard. She had never felt so alone, there were few who understood her pain when she said, "I don't know how much more I can fight." It wasn't something that most could understand. When she called me, I could always tell by the way she answered my normal response "Miss America." She would say her normal "Hi Baby," and the tone of those words would tell me if she was okay or trying to pretend. I could hear the pain and felt the loneliness through her words. There were many calls that afterwards I would rush to visit her or send her a special letter because I was so worried that she was completely done.

There were times that Kristine did wonder if she would be

freed. She knew that the evidence was there to support her innocence but the evidence was always there and she was locked up anyway. She fought the demons of her loss and now fought against the state to prove her innocence. She had won in the Indiana Court of Appeals and felt happy about this victory. Her supporters rejoiced in the victory but Kristine was cautious. She couldn't promise her son that she would be home, only to have his hopes crushed. She knew that her lawyers were not worried about the possible appeal, as they knew that the case was strong and believed completely in her innocence.

The state did appeal and the wait for the Supreme Court began. The struggle to be patient with the slow pace of an overloaded system was a challenge for everyone. Another day in prison was a struggle that Kristine had been living for years now. At least, now she had something to be happy about. She could almost see the light at the end of the tunnel. Yet another birthday came for Trent, he turned 16 in July and was still not sure if his mother would come home. Kristine tried to reassure him that it would be over soon. She tried to keep his spirits up as her own

spirits were getting harder to maintain...the wait lasted until

August.

Chapter Fifteen: 48 hours

August 8, 2012, started as a normal day in prison for Kristine Bunch, but that would soon change when Jane and Hilary called Kristine that afternoon to tell her that her case was upheld by the Indiana Supreme Court. Those words meant that Kristine was no longer a convicted inmate. She was an innocent woman who was being held in prison.

Weeks went by and Kristine was still at the Indiana Women's Prison. She was still waiting despite her win. The prisons day-to-day life should have been over for her, she should have been starting her new life as a free woman. Forty-eight hours had gone past and then some.

With each passing day since the sentence was overturned, she waited patiently to be released. Perhaps to delay her release, Judge Westhafer took a 3-week vacation and the other judge didn't want to release her because it wasn't his case. So, the team of lawyers appealed to the Appellate Court to get a something scheduled. Her team's undeterred fight paid off and the Appellate Court stated she would be released or given a bond whether Judge Westhafer was there or not.

Finally, on August 22, 2012, Kristine was told that she would be going to court and a decision could be made on her release. Decatur County Sherriff deputies would transport Kristine back to Greensburg to have the hearing that could change her life. She was going back to the same court that 17 years before had handed her a sentence of 110 years.

Leaving the prison was bittersweet. She was not being freed into the world but headed back to the Decatur County Jail while a decision would be made if her bond would be reinstated as the prosecutor prepared for a new trial. She said goodbye to the officer and some words of encouragement were spoken as she left in the back of a sheriff's car.

Kristine had to keep her feelings in check. She knew that either way, she had to present herself as a respectable citizen, not the inmate that she had been for the last 17 years. She had to deal with the anger and keep focus on the ultimate dream - her freedom. The hour drive gave her some time to deal with her feelings. She was handcuffed at the wrist and had shackles on her ankles, something that she become accustomed to over the years. The handcuffs and shackles were useless today as running was the last thing on her mind. She had fought this war and she was winning. There was hope.

Kristine knew that she could be released that morning and she also knew that she could be sent back to the jail to await a trial. Her bond was not guaranteed to be given and she could have to spend the next year or more in the county jail as her case shuffled through the judicial system. Her justice could be delayed again and as much as that thought tore her apart, it also motivated her. She knew that she would get her justice which was something that she believed in more than anything. Jail officials didn't even process her in, knowing that she was unlikely to be returning.

Moments before the hearing began, Kristine was led into the courtroom with cameras on her. As one reporter asked her how she was doing, a sheriff's deputy said, "no cameras allowed in the courtroom," leaving Kristine with a smile and nod as she was ushered in the courtroom. She walked into that courtroom with the fears of being captive longer, yet with the excitement that her justice could come that day.

Chapter Sixteen: The Reality of Freedom

Kristine Bunch sat at that table, listening to the words that were spoken and thinking that she would not be freed. She was in a world that was filled with guilt and little innocence, waiting her judgement. Everyone waited with bated breath to see what Kristine's fate would be.

Few understood the fight or the desire to see judgement like her attorneys: Hilary Bowe-Ricks, Jane Raley, Karen Daniel, Kelly Warner and Ron Safer. For 10 years, these lawyers had been working on securing her freedom. They believed in her innocence and were trying to right a wrong. Their hard work had gotten them to this hearing and their fight wasn't over. As much as they wanted Kristine to be freed, they also wanted her name to be cleared.

As composed as she may have been viewed, she was really falling apart. She had long ago mastered the art of controlling her emotions. Seventeen years behind prison walls had taught that lesson. She knew when you smile or even cry, that those emotions showed are judged by others. She had spent years being stoic therefore no one could judge her based on expressions. Even on this morning, where she could gain her freedom, she was cautious of her emotions. She knew the expressions that others found acceptable. She had her head up and was waiting for justice to be spoken.

Kristine had been waiting for this moment, a chance at freedom and she struggled to breathe. In the moments before the judge gave his ruling, she was frozen in time. She was trying to be positive however, the past 17 years had made her disbelieve in things until they are seen. The trust in the system faded over the years, only her belief in her innocence gave her hope. She always believed that the truth would set her free. It was a small-town girl's belief that even the prison couldn't take away.

Judge W. Michael Wilke spoke the words that Kristine had longed to hear. "The defendant is to be released from the Department of Corrections," He said. Her original bond was being reinstated and the judge ordered her release. In the courtroom, there was cheering and sighs of relief for Kristine. The tears flowed as she tried to be composed, but the day that she had long dreamt of was here. She was free - there would be no return to the D.O.C. She would sleep on a real mattress that night and everything was going to be okay.

During Kristine's first moments of freedom she was still handcuffed by the sheriff's department. As she spoke to reporters for the first time you could hear the joy in her first words. When asked "What does this day "mean to you," she simply replied, "It's everything." Her tears of joy flowed as she talked with reporters about her plans and the last 17 years. She did not speak bitterly about her ordeal but with the hope that kept her from giving up.

Kristine walked out of the Decatur County Jail straight into the arms of her mother, Susan and her son, Trent. She was unaware of the many challenges that she would soon face. Her only focus was on rebuilding whatever life she had remaining. She was going to be a mother to Trent and try to build a stronger relationship with him. Her focus was on him.

Before going to her celebration dinner, Kristine gave an exclusive interview to Sandra Chapman with the Indianapolis news station, Channel 13, WTHR. Chapman had done previous interviews with Kristine and there was a level of trust among the women. The interview focused on Kristine's release and how she was feeling. It was too soon for Kristine to know how she was coping. This reality was new and she was just holding on to the belief that she would be okay.

The lawyers took her to Bistro 310, Columbus's nicest restaurant where she celebrated her freedom and had her first few drinks in 17 years. She never tasted food that was so good nor could remember the last time that she was this happy. Beside her she had the one thing that she spent the last 17 years fighting for, her son. Her hard-fought road had brought her to this moment...her first meal out with her son. It was the first of many for her.

Kristine had always envisioned her home coming and how she would walk in the door to some peace. However, even before she arrived at the apartment that her mother and son shared, she could feel the stress – it was more awkward than she had ever felt. Arriving at the apartment didn't help matters. It was a mess and she realized that she had no idea how bad things were where Trent was living. She swallowed her fears and tried to look past the clutter and focus on her son.

Trent quickly introduced Kristine to the world of Facebook and helped her create a page. She knew that she was behind in technology, but she wasn't going to wait to dive into that world. She was free and she wanted to live as normal as possible. She looked at her "new" friends and saw their lives unfold. Looking at pictures and smiling through their joy. She was free to roam Facebook. It was just little thing that most people take for granted daily, but she was enjoying Facebook for the first time.

Kristine slept in a recliner that she could clear off, getting up often to watch her son sleep. A simple thing to most parents, but to her it was everything. She was unsure what to do but she knew that she couldn't live like this. She didn't even have a toothbrush of her own.

When the sun rose, Kristine was up in time to see all its glory. Day two of her freedom was upon her and she was looking forward to a visit with her brother, Michael. She had spoken to Michael the previous night and told him of her frustrations, he readily agreed to come take Kristine to the store. She spent her first hours trying to clean Trent's room, taking more trash bags out of his bedroom than the normal household uses in a month's time. Ten bags of trash and clutter that her son had grown accustomed to. She knew while she was cleaning that she would have to get her son out of this environment. She was angry that her son had been accustomed to this style of living. She worried about the things she found, which included- cigarettes and even "spice," a manufactured form of marijuana. She knew that he was on ADHD medication, but she never knew about the cigarettes and certainly not the "spice."

The reality of her freedom had not fully sunk in, but she knew that she would have to make changes for her son and her. He had just turned 16 in July and she knew that change would be harder for him. She was determined to raise her son to 18, even if her options were limited.

Michael arrived to take Trent and Kristine to dinner at the Texas Roadhouse. The moment that she hugged her brother she felt safe for the first time since her release. He knew her better than anyone and he had grown into a well-rounded man. She knew that her life would never be without Michael again. The pain of missed visits or few visits were gone and replaced with comfort. She felt the security that Michael provided.

After dinner, they dropped Trent off, who didn't want to go shopping. Kristine and Michael went to the outlet mall in Columbus. She needed clothes that weren't the beige prison uniform that she was used to. Michael, having been married for years, helped Kristine, even stopping her from buying all white bras. Most brothers wouldn't advise their big sister on how to shop, but Michael understood that she was used to white and told her to buy one of every color. A simple choice that would change her thinking. It was at that moment that she knew that she knew that she had to color up her new life. Even through the pain that she was experiencing and her disappointments, she was ready to put on her "big girl panties," now in color, and to deal with everything.

Big stores like Walmart were a common thing for most Americans, but for Kristine they were overwhelming. All the different choices of shampoos were amazing to her, how was she supposed to find the right one? Michael told her that they could come every day if that was what it took and she would find the right one. She never expected to feel anxiety over shampoo, but she wasn't good with choices having spent the last 17 years ordering from a form. Thankfully Michael was there to reassure her that they would figure out her hygienic needs and give her the comfort that she hadn't experienced since the judge granted her release.

Kristine stayed at Michael's house that night, having a few drinks and talking with her brother, trying to catch up on his life. Through clicks of toasting glasses, they celebrated her release and looked forward too many more nights. Michael quickly offered Kristine and her son Trent a home.

One of the first places that she needed to go to was her son Tony's grave, somewhere she hadn't been since her conviction in 1996. She needed to visit her son's final resting place and be with him. After arriving at his grave and talking to him for a few moments, she noticed someone taking pictures of her on their cell phone. She quickly left. It was another moment that someone stole from Kristine, a moment that she deserved.

Kristine knew that being a mother meant that you must make decisions that your children didn't want or like. After only a week of living at her mother's apartment, she took Michael up on his offer of moving in with him and his wife, Megan. Trent and she would have their own rooms.

Due to miscommunication and perhaps some lies, Megan and Kristine didn't have a relationship. This did not scare Kristine about living with Michael and Megan, instead she was excited to get to know the woman that had been taking care of her little brother all these years. Almost immediately they connected and the resentment that they may have felt before about each other was gone. The women could drink wine together and talk for hours. They had a lot of similarities beyond their love for Michael.

Kristine may have been walking freely, however legally speaking, she was on bond awaiting her new trial. Her conviction was overturned and she was released on her original bond set in 1995. The trial date was set for February 2013. She knew that she would get a fair trial and she was confident that the lawyers would make sure of that.

The months spent following her release, she was questioning herself and how she handled the wrongful conviction. In a late-night phone call, she asked the question "Do I act like I am bitter?" After a conversation with someone, she started to question herself and look for the answers. She worried that people would see her as bitter even if she had a right to be bitter. Kristine harbored no hard feelings towards the people of the law enforcement, yet she still believed that they should be held accountable for their actions. Kristine didn't want to ever be seen as ungrateful - that was never the case. She was grateful for her freedom, however there were issues that still needed to be addressed. She wanted someone to be accountable for her stolen years with her son and her family. She wanted someone to take responsible for the decision to label the fire as a crime. She needed someone to apologize for the false reports and own up to why the ATF report was altered. Did the fire investigators tell the ATF chemist to alter the report or did the ATF chemist altered the report on his own? She just needed someone to acknowledge that huge injustice that had happened to her and take responsibility for it. She was falsely convicted of the worst crime that a mother could commit. She may have been justified to be bitter against the system, but she believed that wouldn't solve anything.

Another issue that made it harder for Kristine was her lack of money. She did not come home to a job and her struggle to find a job was harder. She was living with her brother Michael along with his wife Megan and her son Trent. Michael tried to ease Kristine's fears about money, however she wanted to take care of herself and her son.

Indiana has no compensation laws for the wrongfully convicted. There is no certificate of Innocence to clear their names and no money to help them rebuild their lives. Only the federal government, District of Columbia, and 30 other states have compensation statutes to assist the innocent as they begin the process of starting over after their release. Indiana is not one of those states so no relief is given to the exonerated. If she had been in Illinois, she would have been eligible to file for a certificate of innocence and would have received $250,000 to help her start her life again. If she were in Texas, she would have received $1.3 million upon her full pardon.

The beginning days of her freedom were rougher than the

prison life that she knew for 17 years. As much as she longed for her freedom, the real world was scarier. In prison, she didn't have the worries that this new life had brought with them. She struggled to find her way with Trent and the belief that she couldn't seem to reach him was devastating for her. They were both trying to live different ways. In many ways, Kristine was trying to reach a young boy that thought he was a man. He had been living a life without rules and boundaries and Kristine was trying to change that. The relationship that she believed was solid leaving the prison was shattering quickly. That was breaking her heart but it encouraged her to fight for him. She quickly took control and set new limits.

When Kristine was released, she looked forward to all her firsts, especially with her son. Just a few months into her journey of freedom, she got to go to a parent-teacher conference. As a mother, I have never gotten as excited for a parent-teacher conference as she was the night before. She texted me pictures and even shared them on her Facebook wall for approval. She wanted to make the right first impression. She already felt that the odds were stacked against her going in there facing a murder trial still. She went in there and won his teachers over. They were not used to a parent taking charge of his success. She was willing to work with his teachers to help Trent succeed. She had just taken the first step in helping Trent graduate and making new limits for him. It was a great feeling to know that she was on the right track to parenting Trent.

Kristine was not naïve when it came to the decision that she would raise Trent upon her release - that was always clear. He was the reason that she was fighting so desperately. He was the reason that she went through the long years of court battles and the long years without any movement on her case. She needed to get to him and she would do whatever it took to raise. However, Trent was angry at her attempts to parent him. He had 16 years to do as he pleased and he was resistant to her parenting. The constant struggle between mother and son caused her more agony. There were sleepless nights and heartbreaking conversations that she had with her child. She had fought so hard to be there for him and it felt as if he was slipping through her fingers.

Kristine knew the list of things that she needed to do was long and would prove to be challenging. She wanted to get her license and quickly went with Michael to get her driver's permit. She passed the test and with Michael in the passenger's side, she took the wheel. Taking the wheel would help ease some of her anxieties and she knew that soon she would get her license and be free to drive around. Michael eagerly helped his sister get comfortable driving again and tried to help her avoid road rage.

Kristine went with her friend Betsy Marks to Chicago to meet with her lawyers to discuss trial preparations. Betsy took her to the North Shore where the water was breathtakingly beautiful. For 17 years, she only saw barbed-wire and fences. Standing there looking at the beauty of the water, for the first time since her release, she found peace. The water brought a cleansing within Kristine that made her feel less damaged. She stood there quietly and smiled through the tears that lined her face. For a moment, the water had calmed her wounded heart. Ron Safer took Kristine to a restaurant in Willis Tower, which overlooked the city's skyline. The beauty of Chicago gave her a sense of peace. She was mesmerized by the skyline that stretched over the city. In that moment, she knew she needed a fresh start. She knew that she wanted to start over and that would happen in Chicago. She was at peace here and she wanted a chance to keep it. She didn't know how it was going to happen but she had something that she wanted. She needed a fresh start in a new city and state.

Kristine's first Christmas at home, she struggled with celebrating. Christmas was always just another day for her while in prison. She felt more pressure than anything. The outside world celebrated by decorating their homes and trees elaborately. It wasn't something that Kristine had done over the last 17 Christmases and she was overwhelmed at the thought.

Her first Christmas home, her life was still in limbo and she was still facing a retrial for the arson charge. Along with trial looming over her head, she was unprepared for Christmas. She felt too broken and the tradition of Christmas festivities made her realize just how much she had lost. She wasn't there to set up the tree with Trent, or get him his first bike on Christmas. Christmas in all its glory did not feel the same. It was another reminder of how much she had lost in the last 17 years. She bought gifts out of necessity and so that other persons feelings would not be hurt. Still, she wasn't a Grinch either, she proudly decorated the outside of Michael's house with an inflatable Santa.

December 18, 2012, brought news that the Decatur County Prosecutor dropped all charges against Kristine. The relief was short-lived and the reality that they could recharge her loomed over her. Some of her supporters saw this as an early Christmas gift, to Kristine this was just another way that her justice would be delayed. Kristine wanted that second trial, she needed to hear the words "Not guilty." She deserved to be fully exonerated from the charges and have her name cleared after years of living with that first verdict. She knew that a second jury would have never convicted her with all the new findings of the case. The dismissal of the charges didn't give her comfort, it only fueled her quest for justice. Her conviction had been reversed but she didn't feel exonerated. The prosecutor did not drop the charges when she was released and he gave no reason for his intent to retry Kristine. The prosecutor was still planning on a retrial for the 1995 fire. He still believed that Kristine was guilty and was actively looking for a fire investigator that specialized in fire science to go against the experts that Kristine's defense team had readily on hand. Kristine believes that he would never change his mind about her innocence; no matter what evidence is presented.

Another reality hit her that morning when she learned that her mother was behind some of the interview requests. Kristine went over to her mother's apartment and she gave an interview. She was still struggling when she got the call that the media were there. She was upset to learn of her mother's involvement, but it was just one more thing to add to the list. She told the reporter that she was grateful and held no ill feelings towards the state for "doing their jobs." However inside she was a mess. She didn't want to talk to the reporters, nor did she want her mother to speak to the media. She wanted silence. She wanted to talk when she was ready. She wanted to let the reality that she was truly free and not awaiting a new trial to sink in. She just wanted to move on.

Kristine's first few months were some of the hardest days for her. She dreamt of coming home to her son and while she knew that there would be adjustments, she was floored by his behaviors. He was so used to doing his own thing that he baulked at his mother's requests. Sometimes to the point where Michael would get involved, which then involved the police. Trent was trying to hold on to his old life and refused to meet Kristine in the middle.

She had just fought for 17 years to get to him and she was losing him. True to form, she stood her ground believing that she wouldn't give up. She knew that she could get through to him and they would have that mother-son relationship that she longed for. The more she fought, the harder it got. Kristine had to make hard decisions that broke her spirit even more. She was quickly becoming a broken vase that she worried could never be repaired.

The decision to put Trent into a treatment center was Kristine's attempt to help Trent. She wanted to get him off all the medications that he had been taking since he was young. A decision that Kristine never supported and now she could see that she was right to be concerned about the harmful medications. It was the hardest thing that she had to do when she left Trent at the center and she spent 20 minutes crying in her car before driving the hour back to Michael's house. Her mind raced and she questioned if she was making the best decision for Trent.

Kristine's first Christmas approached rapidly, with many requests to join her family's get togethers, it was all that she could do not to turn her phone off and avoid the many requests. The anxiety that she felt at just the thought of being surrounded by her family was too much for her. Instead of a huge family dinner, she joined Michael and Megan on a trip to Mexico. On the beach, she could feel the air of the ocean and see the beauty that it had. She read a book and sipped a sweet cocktail, her surroundings. She had five days to celebrate and enjoy the ocean. It was the greatest Christmas gift that she could have received. It was no added pressure and she could just breathe.

Returning to reality, she quickly started planning for her move to Chicago which was her only New Year's resolution even though she always considered resolutions to be silly. "If you are going to make a change, don't wait until a certain date, just do it, she said." She knew that the move wouldn't be easy, however her release wasn't easy either. Life for Kristine was never easy, it was just another cross that she had to bear. She had to fight harder than most. She started to consider possible connections that might help her make the transition.

In April, she attended the annual Innocence Conference in North Carolina, an annual event that brought exonerees and legal teams together. It is an event that brings old and new exonerees to one location so they can support each other. All her expenses were paid by the Innocence Conference, which is something that is done for every new exoneree for the first year. She attended without worries about her financial situation and solely focused on being around people who understood her struggle.

Kristine found this to be helpful to her newfound freedom. She was surrounded by people who understood her pain and could relate to the challenges that even her best support people couldn't understand. The weekend event allowed her to be herself, allowing her to talk about her experiences without feeling judged. She could relate to fellow exonerees and learn new information due to the different seminars that were going on around her.

After the conference, it was business as usual for Kristine. She went back to work at the gas station and made plans for Trent to come home. She was preparing for her move to Chicago, which she wanted to be by her 40th birthday in October. She had a goal and with every goal, she was determined to make it come true.

She started to reach out to connections within the university and the innocence community. It was that community that she truly felt a part of. They were able to relate to her in ways that most people can't even understand. Too many times, prisoners, innocent or even guilty, get lost after their release, which can lead to repeat offenses or even suicide.

Too many times people judge based on what they hear and not what is reality. The reality is that life after prison is harder than prison life was. The best way to explain it is this... In prison, you have a roof over your head with three meals a day and you do not have to pretend that everything is good. You get lost in the daily routines and look at the outside world as picture perfect... never imagining how cold and bleak the world really is. Every prisoner can tell at least one thing that they missed the most. For me, it was McDonald's and the ability to wake up and go outside in the morning. For Kristine, it was Trent. She could envision watching him sleep or taking him to an amusement park where they would ride all the rides together. However, after being released you must worry about bills and more importantly, you must look at your relationships for what they are. Kristine was dealt this painful lesson, too harshly and too early into her release. She believed that she and Trent would have challenges, but never imagined a life that he didn't want her in. She was heartbroken and even as the relationship was worsening, she was fading into the background quickly. The only thing that she knew to do was to fight for her dreams. Chicago was her dream and she knew that she would need to cross the state border to achieve a different life for herself.

The hardest part of deciding to start over in Chicago for Kristine was accepting that no matter how hard she tried, she had lost her son, Trent. Although, she had done everything for him even beyond normal measures, she had lost him. Those moments are forever gone and she could never get them back. Her vision that she had as she left the prison that August day of getting her family back was slowly shattered over the year. Her teenage son Trent had a mom and it wasn't Kristine - it was her mom Susan.

It wasn't that she didn't plan on taking him. She spent hours looking at two-bedroom apartments in the perfect school districts and looking for the best spots to take him. She dreamed of rebuilding her life over and making new memories with the son that she fought so hard to get home to. The choice was not hers, but rather Trent's, who after years of his grandma raising him, decided his loyalty lay with her and not Kristine. As much as that truth hurt, Kristine had to move forward and try to rebuild her life. Her move to Chicago had to be done for her to see if she had any chance to have a normal life again. No matter how hard it was to say goodbye to Trent, she had to make that leap alone.

Living alone didn't scare Kristine as she had felt alone for many years. She wanted to change her zip code and hopefully find another piece of her soul that was lost. The move to Chicago was her opportunity to start over and rebuild whatever life that she had left. Like the legendary bird the Phoenix that Kristine has always been fascinated with, she had to rise from the ashes and soar.

Chapter Seventeen: Starting Over Again

Turning 40, Kristine Bunch took a huge leap into the world. She moved to Chicago, Illinois on her birthday and into a small one-bedroom apartment in the middle of the suburb of Evanston. Her apartment was her first home that she would be living in since Tony's death. The apartment was small, however to Kristine it was charming. She had enough space for her belongings and for all the many gifts that others had given her since her release. One of the first things that she did was unpack her photos of her sons, Trent and Tony.

Along with her was her brother and sister-in–law, they moved all her belongings into the apartment. They put together the different rooms, even as they put things away. Kristine knew that she would change it later. She could do those things now. She was not living in a cell anymore, it was more space than she had in 17 years. She had a bedroom that was separate from her bathroom, she even had a dining room. Even the struggle of getting her couch, a gift from her brother, up the four flights of stairs was not a bother. Kristine was beyond happy to be starting over in the "windy city."

Kristine went to Chicago with a transfer within Speedway, although the job soon fell apart. The position that she was transferring into was not available. Here she was 250 miles from home and she was faced with being unemployed. Anyone else would have been deterred, but not Kristine. She quickly picked up some temporary positions with Northwestern University while looking for a permanent position. She knew that she was meant to be in Chicago. Thankfully, her rent was being paid by the landlord for 6 months and adjusted for the next 6 months. That generosity helped calm Kristine's fear of failing in this new city.

Kristine's new apartment was in the center of Evanston- a small suburb just north of Chicago. It was walking distance to the local post offices and many different stores. It was on the fourth floor that overlooked the city's beauty. Her door was near the apartment building's fire escape stairs, which is where she went to have that occasional cigarette to calm her nerves. Her apartment was minutes away from the Evanston campus of Northwestern University. She was centrally located, which made it a better location for her. It was a dream come true.

Kristine's first Christmas in her apartment, there was no tree as she still wasn't really feeling that traditional yet. However, she proudly displayed her plant that she had managed to keep alive. Its limbs shimmered like diamonds and it was the most beautiful thing I had ever seen. I always knew that the normal Christmas traditions would be harder for her, but seeing that plant gave me hope. Hope that one day she would want trees, decorating the house, or just enjoy the shopping. Seeing that plant make me realize that her version of Christmas was different. She seemed to enjoy the plant as much as I did my tree that I always put up on the day after Thanksgiving. It brought a joy that I haven't ever seen and reminded of me of her journey.

Kristine soon found a job at Rivers Casino in Des Plaines, Illinois, a 30-minute drive from her apartment. She had to go through the normal background check and that caused her some anxiety. What if something came up that would prevent the casino from hiring her? She knew that she would be an excellent employee as she had always had a great work ethic. Finally, she received the offer of employment: 3rd shift security at the Casino. She had an income and at least some of her money issues would be solved.

Kristine was still working for Northwestern in temporary positions as they became available. There were weeks that she was lucky to sleep for more than three hours a day between her casino job, temporary assignments and still maintaining her relationships all around. She wanted to be on top of everything in her life. She was also was doing speaking engagements. She was building her connections and maintaining even though the pain of her freedom was costly.

Kristine was overjoyed by her freedom and was thankful for every day that she was freed. However, the pain was still there. She still had to deal with everyday life along with her grief and the hard days that she spent stuck behind bars for a crime that she didn't commit. The depression was hard and even small things sent her into a tailspin. Any loss was just a reminder of all the losses that she had already been through. She was struggling with everyday decisions and telling others would only hurt them. She wasn't looking for pity, just a listening ear. She knew that she was strong, but there were many days that she didn't feel strong. By this point, Kristine had accepted the fact that she needed professional help.

Kristine met Faith*[15], a local Chicago therapist and began to see her on a weekly basis. She was nervous about starting this process but knew that she needed to be able to talk someone who was completely unbiased. As much as she loved her family and friends, she was scared that the ugly truth of what she felt would be too much for them to handle. She felt the pain over and over each moment of the day. She wanted to express herself without fear or judgement, something that she still felt. She could

---

[15] (not real name; changed to protect identify)

walk in that office and unload all her issues, leaving a piece of the pain behind.

It wasn't easy and it took everything in her to speak but she was finally, able to speak all of her truth. The things that were bottled up for years were flowing out of her. The more she told Faith, the more that Kristine grew.

Finally, in April of 2014, a permanent position opened at Northwestern's Chapel, as an administration assistant and Kristine quickly applied. She was thrilled when she was offered the position which would give her benefits and a pay raise. She was equally pleased with her new surroundings. The building had two chapels: the Millar chapel which could sit 700 people and the Veil chapel that seated 125. The beauty was captured in the stained glass and the wooden chancel. There were other areas of hidden beauty like the outdoor sitting area that was in the middle of the building. It was open, yet closed off from the rest of the world. Kristine felt a peace sitting on the patio just breathing the sweet air that fresh spring brought. Her life was starting to feel different.

She was learning to accept what she couldn't change.

Making more money also meant that Kristine could move to a bigger apartment. She found the perfect two-bedroom apartment in Chicago's Rogers Park area, which was just minutes from the North Shore (which was part of the reason that Chicago was home). Walking into the foyer, you were immediately greeted by the hardwood floors that covered throughout the quaint apartment. Her new kitchen was more spacious with the dining room that was connected. She even had another bathroom that included a jetted tub. She felt beyond blessed to have her new home.

Kristine began the process of having a baby in December of 2014. She was given little hope due to her age of 41, and the condition of reproduction organs. Inside the prison, there were no yearly checkups and even if you needed a regular checkup those were not adequate. She was fighting against her biological clock and years of lack of proper healthcare. It was a dream that she had and was not giving up on - she wanted to be a mother. She wanted another chance to see all the moments that she lost with Trent and all the moments that Tony did not get to have. She longed to struggle with her newborn and watch him or her grow. She still had love to give as a mother.

Christmas day brought more pain for Kristine. Jane Raley lost her heroic battle with cancer. She had spent the past 14 years fighting for prisoners that were wrongfully convicted with the Bluhm Legal Clinic. Her loss was felt throughout the university and the innocence community and especially for Kristine. To this day, she still has Jane's number in her cell phone and sometimes when she dials the 847-area code Jane's number pop ups, which brings an instant smile. Kristine will always be grateful that Jane helped her when she needed it the most, but mostly she is just grateful that she was a friend too.

Along with a new team of lawyers, People's Law Office and the Bluhm Legal Clinic of the Northwestern University School of Law, Kristine filed a lawsuit against two former Indiana State Fire Marshal's, Bryan Frank and James Skaggs. The suit alleges that they jumped to conclusions from the start of their investigation, which resulted in 17 years stolen from Kristine. It also states that the defendants hid evidence that would have resulted in no charges ever being filed against Kristine. A report was fabricated to show that arson was the cause of the fire and it was not accidental. A simple act that took a grieving mother away from society to a prison sentence that took much more than her freedom.

Kristine's lawsuits are about much more than money. There is no amount that would erase the years of loss that she felt. It is another way that Kristine shows that she's a fighter. She is up against Goliath, yet she is standing strong. She knows that the battle may last years and still result in no gain for her personally. It may be thrown out, like so many before her. It is unlikely that she will ever receive an apology from anyone since they are too busy blaming each other. While they are blaming each other, Kristine is looking for answers. She needs to know why someone decided that they had right to frame her and take

17 years. Her fight has never been about money, but rather justice. She needs someone to acknowledge her fight for justice and apologize for the pain that was inflicted on her. She needs the system to make changes so that others won't have to lose their lives. No one should ever have to spend a night as a wrongfully convicted prisoner, let alone the average of 14 years that it takes to get their conviction overturned.

Kristine may have not harbored ill feelings toward anyone, but she still needed someone to be held accountable. It is unclear who made the decision to alter that report, or why it was changed. It could have been the fire investigators that advised the ATF chemist to change the report. If that is true, then the chemist testified knowing that he was lying, which in the court of law is perjury. If it was one of the fire investigators, then they also knew that they were lying to the jury. In the state of Indiana, they are immune to prosecution and per the plaintiffs of Kristine's lawsuit, they believe that Kristine should not be able to sue. They also maintain that these investigators and chemist are not classified as state or federal employees.

This issue brings up an interesting question. If the investigators and chemist are not classified as state or federal employees, shouldn't they have to face an investigation regarding their lies? Since neither state nor federal plaintiffs want to acknowledge them as employees, then that should also be the reason why the altered report should be properly investigated. The altered report was given as the only piece of evidence at her trial and possibly could have been the reason that 12 jurors found Kristine guilty. If they are not liable for a financial payment in the lawsuit, then they should be investigated as they did to Kristine. It can be proven that they all lied on the stand in front of the jury that convicted her.

Committing perjury is a serious offense, especially in Kristine's case. It allowed 17 years to be stolen from her. It took everything, but the worst thing it took was her innocence. That innocence of being in the process of the judicial system, the innocence of believing the best of people, and her innocence of being a free woman. She was forced to view the world differently and learn to become a person that she never imagined possible. It took her sense of being able to understand why people framed others, something that she could have never imagined possible before the fire. She grew up believing that they were protected and the fact that someone could ever frame her was unfathomable. She also lost the mind of an innocent woman, where she could never imagine eating the dinner table with a drug dealer, murderer, and con artist as a normal routine. She never dreamed that those same people would motivate her to fight the system. Not every prisoner should be there and the need for reform is needed in sentencing laws.

She had to deal with her anger over what the investigators did to her for 17 years. She was forced to look at her relationships and wonder if they were out to harm her. She was forced to see the world differently and see the bad qualities. She was forced to live in a world where she was surrounded by criminals that changed her to her core. They changed the way she lived her life.

Before her time was stolen, she was a mother that lived for her son and saw the good in the world. She had little time for drama. Now she was always on guard, waiting for that moment that she would have to protect herself. She had to become a harder person to survive the fences of I.W.P. and other prisoners. She had to hide her pain behind a smile that was truly a lie. Now she can barely trust anyone and the ones who she does trust, have proven their loyalty. They are the ones that she can turn to in a crisis and know that there is no judgement or rejection.

The innocence can never be given back to Kristine. She will always feel that she is being judged by others. She knows that there are people who believe that she isn't innocent, but rather simply found a way to get around the legal system. She can no longer look at justice as blind as she has seen how those investigators could frame her for a crime that never was. She still holds the pain of everything she lost in those 17 years. She can't have back her life. Her life will never be as it was before that night.

Kristine would have likely survived Tony's tragic death. It may have motivated her to promote fire safety that could have saved another mother's child. Who knows? They took that from young Kristine. She could have fought for better awareness of the hazards that trailers have. Maybe she would have formed a grief support program to help others. Knowing how much compassion she has even after all the losses in her life, Kristine would have done something great to help others. She has a soft spot for helping people and even through her own pain, she is amazing.

No amount of money can give her back those missing years. They vacated her sentence, but they can't vacate her prison sentence for a crime that she was innocent of. They can never take away the pain that she felt every night as she laid on concrete and cried because she missed her son and family. They can't simply undo the people that died while she was locked up and give her the proper goodbye that she deserved.

Kristine understands why the jurors found her guilty. That altered report was strong evidence. Too bad that it was a fabricated report, a malicious stroke of a pen writing two simple

numbers that changed that fire at 999 S. Lake McCoy, lot 60 from

an accidental fire to arson. An act that costed Kristine everything,

including raising her son. That was her reality for 17 years, one

month, two weeks and three days. The biggest shame is that

those investigators cannot be tried for falsifying that report. They

are protected by laws that protect law enforcement officials from

prosecution. They could frame a young mother who had just lost

everything that ever mattered to her - her son. They took her

worst tragedy and turned it into the ultimate nightmare. There

will never be a trial to convict them and take away their freedom.

William Kinard is deceased, Bryan Frank works for an insurance

company and James Skaggs, as of 2013, was still an investigator

for the Indiana State Fire Agency.

In December 2015, Kristine spoke at a seminar presented

by Kane County, Illinois, along with three other exonerees. This

was not the first talk that she had given, in fact, by this point she

had done more than a dozen talks. Her motivation was still the same, to try to help a wounded system. A system that needed to provide more resources for public defenders, especially for the scientific cases like hers.

Kristine made the decision to share her story, hoping that other wrongfully convicted people would be saved from years of being imprisoned. On the stage, you could see her dedication to the cause and there wasn't a dry eye in the room. She spoke about her conviction and then challenged the audience to help fix the broken system that has wrongfully convicted so many. She challenged them to do more and with each speaking event that followed, the challenge increased. Her words were full of hope for change.

Although her words were full of hope, there is still a sadness that can be heard in her words. The loss of her sons is vividly clear and where there was hope for the future, the sadness of the lost past was ever present. She spoke for 45 minutes and the look of composure still came through. The audience didn't see the agony of relieving her past and the damage that each talk brought. She was still standing, however the pain felt as raw as the days that she was living the pain. She was fighting for justice and for those still lost in the system, branded a criminal by the courts.

The after-party was a Christmas party for the defender's office at a local bar. It was in the back room, set up nicely to reflect the season. Kristine and the other speakers, along with their guests, shared a few drinks. As the drinks came, the stories came as did the wishes for change. It was no longer a formal setting but the issues of the wrongfully convicted were still spoken about. There were stories of hope and other stories of despair that many there could relate to. What amazed me the most was the heartache of these public defenders and investigators. Their pain was as real as the exonerees and to see how much passion they had was an amazing experience. There was laughter and even some tears. Kristine shared a drink with the group and as she looked at her glass, the pain was still there. She still had the same cross to bear, her pain was still there, even at the bottom of the glass.

2016 started out different for Kristine as she was planning on moving back to Indiana in June. Many, including her employer at the university, didn't know this. It was a secret except for her circle of personal people. She wasn't moving from Chicago for the same reason that she left Indiana. She was going home to be closer to her family. Michael was already busy looking for the perfect house that he would share with his sister and Kristine was wrapping up her business in Chicago. Chicago had given Kristine the courage to fight in her own state and it was time to see how she could help. She was already working with an innocence clinic based out of Indiana University. She had dreams of getting new bills passed in Indiana concerning the innocent. She would love to see a compensation bill passed, however even a certificate of innocence in Indiana would be great.

Epilogue: Hard Road Home

Today Kristine has returned to Indiana. She lives about 30 minutes outside of Indianapolis. The decision to come home was not something Kristine made overnight. She spent two and half years building her life in Chicago and was genuinely happy living in Chicago. Part of her heart will always be in the "Windy City." However, Kristine felt it was time to try to reform Indiana's laws to better help future and current wrongfully convicted inmates. Kristine's heart is pure even after all she has survived.

Kristine returned to Indiana with hopes of having a position working in the Indiana University Innocence Clinic, however funding was not possible. She still maintains a relationship with Fran, the lawyer that heads the clinic and still helps by reviewing cases and asking lawyers to assist. She does it all on a volunteer basis, as she believes that she can see things that might help others gain their freedom. One of the problems with smaller clinics are resources. Investigators or new scientific testing is costly. Kristine knows that her own defense was expensive. Just the lawyers alone could have been over a million dollars. Then when you add the experts, it could have easily have been over $2 million. Thankfully, she had lawyers and even experts that gave her pro-bono hours to aid in her case. She will never be able to repay the money, even if she does win her lawsuit. Some costs will always outweigh the repayment. She knows that there are many innocent people still left rotting in their prison cells. With each passing day, they too are losing hope of their freedom. When another inmate is released, the lawyers move to the next case and the cost of freedom grows. Kristine knows this struggle and wants to help in any way possible, even if is on her free time. She knows that there are not enough lawyers and investigators to help all the innocent people still lost in the system. Her mission is to help others come home too.

Miss America has more grace and determination than any other women in the world. She trains for years sometimes from birth, entering pageants and losing sometimes. But the goal is to be Miss America. Kristine Bunch may never have the diamond-encrusted crown that matches the title, but she deserves one. She has showed how a woman who should be hateful, bitter and angry can still offer encouraging words to someone who killed their own child or family member. Kristine showed compassion to those who did not know what compassion was. She has shown compassion to those who are lost in a system that wasn't built for rehabilitation or constructed to make a better person. The systems were built to house inmates for a paycheck and try to make the prisoner a better citizen upon release. If you believe that prison offers a new way out... you would be mistaken. There are few programs that are helping inmates with life after prison. Just like the birds that fly into the prison they will never be the same. However, the birds don't realize that they're just flying into open space as the women watch and wish that they could fly out too. A bird is simply flying into a prison yard, not realizing that it is a prison and each woman is aware of the cage that surrounds them daily. Trapped inside the fences, Kristine did the impossible -

she learned how to fly. She rose from her horrible conviction, and rose to a level that made her a better person than most. She walked the hardest stage, being wrongfully convicted.

Kristine can stand on a stage and capture an audience, making them feel her pain. She stands up there, pouring out her heart and pain, silently saying a prayer that at least one person will be saved from years of pain due to a wrongful conviction. She is hoping that she says something that will motivate someone to help their client from the years of misery that she suffered. She doesn't talk about her pain to make herself feel better. It doesn't help her, in fact it hurts her. What the audience doesn't see is who she is after and the struggle that her pain has become. She has her freedom but she isn't yet free.

Kristine came back to Indiana with a new project: JustIS 4 JustUS. A non-profit organization that was founded by Juan Rivera, another exoneree, which continues to fight the war to help the innocent. The organization is designed to help other exonerees as they are released back into society. Both Kristine and Juan know the struggles that are faced for the newly released and they believe that money should not be one of them. They hope to be an organization that is built on community support and grow it into a larger support system.

Support is something that Kristine also has provided to other exonerees. She traveled to Oklahoma after a fellow exoneree was struggling to deal with life outside of prison. Kristine could provide support in a special way. Both women had lost their child and were falsely convicted of the deaths. She went there to just listen and help her learn ways to deal with the added stress that they both faced daily. She could be there to motivate her without any judgement. Kristine has shown over and over that she will go the extra mile to help. That is another way that she is changing the course of how the innocent will overcome their trials. Even if sharing her own painful experiences increases her anxiety and causes her pain to increase.

The one thing that I have noticed over the years, Kristine struggles after talks or events that are centered on the cause. She knows that she is fighting to make a difference, but there are those times when I wonder at what cost. The pain never leaves and the amount of stress increases, however she is still standing. For her, that means she must keep fighting. She knows that the cause needs her, because there are too many innocent people still fighting for someone to even believe in their innocence. She fights with courage and determination for those who cannot.

The hardest part is the past can never be rewritten for Kristine. Her conviction has changed her forever. There will always be something missing in her life and it will affect her daily. The prayer is that pain will lessen over time. But it isn't only her pain that affects her. Trent will never know what it is like to have his mother outside the prison. For 16 years of his life, his contact with his mother was inside prison walls. No number of visits or parties that he got to be with his mother can ever replace having his mother there when he had a bad dream or his first day of school. He will never know what it is like to have other siblings. He didn't get to see how hard his mother worked. No one will never know how far she would have succeed in her career or if she would have attended college for a more lucrative career. Trent was cheated out of knowing his mother daily. If she could become the amazing person that she did surviving her wrongful conviction, I know that she could done more. She became a woman that is looking to make a difference in as many lives as possible. She is dedicated to preventing any innocent person from having to spend another day in prison. If you look at the journey, it is not about how it ended, but how it's going, because the end of a battle is never the end, the war still rages.

The state took away much more than her freedom - they took away her right to be a mother, sister, aunt, and a much-needed friend for 17 years. They also took her right to properly grieve for Tony and replace that grief with different emotions. They took everything that Kristine wanted in life. They took her right to grieve the loss of her son. Is there any amount of money that could begin to cover her losses? Close your eyes and imagine that your son was gone, you are wrongfully convicted, you lose the right to be a mother to your newborn and you lose important people in your life. Can you imagine that pain? How would you feel? What would be justice?

No matter how hard it has gotten, Kristine has tried to maintain a relationship with Trent, the son that should have been raised by her, not her mother. It has been a struggle though and she has had to learn how to live out in the real world twice. Once when she was released and then again without Trent being her sole focus. She has faced the world feeling all alone in the sadness that had become her reality. She has worked hard to change her perspective in daily life. There are times that she feels on top of a mountain and in control, just for life to throw her a curveball and she struggles to climb up again. The loss of Tony is unimaginable, but the loss of Trent was cruel and deliberately taken from her, simply unforgivable. The only thing that she was fighting for was taken from her and she has learned to live for herself. She lost Trent also with her wrongful conviction.

Kristine still has dreams of becoming a mother again as she

feels that it is her destiny. Throughout the years, after many failed attempts, she hasn't lost that dream. She still believes that motherhood is still part of her future. She wants the chance to have another sweet baby that she can raise and love as she loves her boys, Tony and Trent. She is not looking for a replacement for either, just another child to give all this love she still should give. Who knows if she would have never been wrongfully imprisoned, Trent might have had another brother or even a couple of sisters.

In the name of justice, all cases need to be looked at with clear and detailed knowledge and understanding of the law. In Kristine's case, rush to judgement cost her everything. It took her freedom, the chance to properly grieve her son, and the chance to raise her newborn son. She should have been there to rock him to sleep, or see him off on the first day of school. She was blessed to get weekly visits, but she should have been the one raising him.

Why? Why did Kristine have to lose 17 years of her life for a tragic accident? Where is the justice that Kristine deserved years ago, where is the truth? You can't simply say sorry for the injustice that Kristine suffered. A tragic accident turned into a nightmare for one young mother. Although an apology would help Kristine see that the state at least felt some remorse for stealing 17 years from her.

Since Kristine's release, she has been on a mission to help spread the message and raise awareness for those still fighting. Along with her speaking engagements and filing her lawsuits, she has been actively involved in helping other exonerees and trying to change the future for new exonerees. She spoke in front of Wyoming legislators in November 2016, telling her story in hopes of changing the two-year time limit for new evidence and getting a compensation law passed to help other exonerees when they are freed. Even though there is little hope that Indiana will pass a similar law, she was spreading the message to anyone that will listen. She was hoping that by sharing her personal story of sadness and heartaches that another person will be saved from that pain.

One could not blame Kristine if she just chose to live a

quiet life and move on from her wrongful conviction. No one would blame her for choosing a life without having a spotlight, but then she would not be being herself. She chooses to fight so others don't have to fight as hard. She hopes for an easier road for the next freed man or woman. It is estimated that at least 120,000 of the 2.4 million people who are incarnated in America's prisons are innocent according to the Innocence Project. However, in 2015, the highest number of exonerations was set at 149, not even 1% of the projected innocent. Kristine knows that she may be speaking to deaf ears at some events, but she hopes that she can spark at least one more person's interest. She chooses to continue to fight and believe that the war against the Judicial system is winning more and more battles. Those winning battles are changing more lives and helping others.

Late one Saturday night, Kristine sat around a metal table surrounded by family and friends trying to celebrate her brother's birthday. There was a fire in the pit in the yard that she faithfully had been adding wood to. As it burns Kristine watched the fire, yet remained involved in the many conversations going on around her. One conversation was that Michael is a workaholic while another conversation is that Kristine should cut that dead tree in the middle yard. Both conversations going on with her input, they both surround her and for a moment, Kristine looks in control. There is a distant look in her eyes though, as if she is lost in her own thoughts. As the fire burns out, guests start to leave and the conversations move into the kitchen inside. One conversation brings tears among some - some who have known Kristine for years and some who have met her recently. It is a moment of clarity, you can see the final truth of Kristine's ordeal. There will always be a mountain of pain that she must climb daily, but she will. When she does, she will be a little stronger. However, there will always be that mountain.

With each new day, Kristine must make the decision to choose happiness. Her experiences as a mother, sister, prisoner and as a woman that was wrongly imprisoned could have left her bitter and angry at the world but she chooses to be happy. It is a constant battle finding happiness during her fight and finding that happiness is hard at times. Her world has been filled with such sorrow that she could be sad, however her amazing smile still shines.

With the same grace and poise that you see in the Miss America pageants, Kristine fights through her life now. She continues to amaze others by her strength and courage. Like the Phoenix bird, she has risen from the ashes, more beautiful and strong as she flies through trying to help stop as many wrongful convictions as she can. No longer defined by Indiana's standards of guilt, Kristine has broken the chains, trading them for wings. As she soars into the unknown, her quest is to find justice for others who are still chained to injustice.

Author's Note:

As Kristine's "sister," I have experienced her journey. I watched as she fought through the court system and watched as she struggled with freedom. I lived through the rejections, the defeats, her cries of sorrow and the good things that happened. I saw how she was strong even when she thought she was too weak to continue to fight. I also saw how she hid a happy person inside, she never tried to hide her joy, only her sorrow. She never wanted to be a bitter person as she had every right to become. I watched as she told everyone else that she was fine when I knew that she hadn't slept for a week because her dorm was so hot.

Living it, I thought I was prepared for the journey that I embarked on when I started my journal of her story. I thought that I had experienced everything that I needed to be able to write her story. I started my journal with a list of visions for her book. I wanted to be able to show the world the woman, who despite her situation, raised a lost teenager into a beautiful person who even I was proud of. I wanted to show the world all the good that I saw in her and why she has always been my Miss America.

When I was a child, I used to watch the Miss America. I watched as the most beautiful women would walk across the stage, smiling and waving as they walked around in painful high heels. I wondered about their backstories as I never took people at face value due to my own childhood. There was one Miss America who caught my attention and I dreamed of finding someone in my life to be a real Miss America to me. I knew that it wasn't about the beauty but the passion that these women had.

I started calling Kristine Miss America because of that passion. When I met Kristine, she had every right to be a loner in the walls of I.W.P. and I saw how much she missed her sons, yet she was still there to offer words of comfort to other prisoners who were struggling. I watched as she tried to make someone's day better. To me in those first days, she was the Miss America who I saw in those pageants. Her grace for others was amazing and her determination to get to her son made me realize that she was the best woman that I ever had in my life. She chose me to be her little sister.

There were times that I sat at my computer and cried at how deep her pain was. I was naïve when I thought I could express her pain in writing. I cried thinking how my typed words might hurt her all over again and I would be responsible for those tears. I would text her my fears, hoping that she would back out. I wanted to be released from that possible betrayal that I felt I was creating.

However, Kristine would call me and assure me that I wouldn't hurt her - that she had already lived through it. She challenged me to be true to myself. Her words of encouragement and courage made me realize that her faith in me was my driving force. I wrote with all the love that she had ever given me. I wrote with the hope that readers would read her story and realize how she was truly Miss America. I wanted my readers to see how amazing Kristine Bunch is. I wrote knowing that there would be tears but there would also be hope for change seen in her incredible journey.

I learned more about the person that I called my big sister for the last 20 years and how incredible she really is. I saw how her wrongful conviction made her even stronger than I ever knew or even understood. I learned how she could have survived - they didn't succeed in taking everything from her. Her soul was too strong and even though it was badly bruised, her soul was still there. She had enough faith to can enjoy the small things in life.

Throughout this experience, I find myself questioning how much I ever understood about the law and how our system works. I found myself questioning my own conviction and looking through the law through Kristine's journey, I understand her passion for the innocent. I see why it is America's problem and why we all should be fighting. We must demand justice for all, even if the crime is so horrible that we do not understand it. We must demand fair justice instead of the justice that is brought on by law enforcement looking for an easy conviction. There are so many areas that demand focus and even we don't see the change in our generation. Maybe it will be enough that the next generation will see the changes. There are too many innocent people suffering injustice. I dream of a world that justice is for all, regardless of race, sex, or the size of their bank account.

In Memoriam of Jane Ellen Raley

Jane was a passionate advocate for the falsely accused and an attorney dedicated to fighting injustice. During her years at Northwestern University Law School's Center on Wrongful Convictions, Jane was instrumental in the exoneration of 11 inmates from prison.

Jane not only exonerated me but she became my mentor, friend and trusted loved one. She encouraged every hope and dream I held in my heart and she assisted me in trying to make them a reality. Jane knew that the biggest dream in my heart was to build a relationship with my son. For my son's 17th birthday, I took him to Chicago to celebrate. Jane invited me to her home where she had prepared a picnic, blankets, chairs and candles for us to take to an outdoor concert close to her home. The experience was magical for all of us.

Jane passed away on December 25th, 2014. There will never be enough words to describe all that Jane meant to me. I still feel her loss every day but I still feel the love, encouragement and insight that she gave to me. She continues to be a driving force within my heart.

Fighting for my freedom was one of the biggest battles I faced. I am grateful that I had a warrior like Jane Raley as my general.

Kristine Bunch

Acknowledgements:

To my husband, John- I am so grateful that you showed me a love that soars and conquers all. You have given me the support needed to write this book. Thank you for always believing in me and encouraging me to reach for the stars.

To my wonderful children- I could have finished this book sooner but you stole my time to chase the ice cream truck or play in the park. I am thankful for the lessons that you continue to teach me- you have given me more of a reason to follow my dreams. I love you first!

To Megan- I am beyond thankful that you are in my life. You are much more than my best friend- you're the little sister that I never knew I needed.

To Ruth Fuller- Thank you for showing me another side to writing. The wisdom that you shared with me makes me a better writer. Thank you for your help in completing this book!

To my Miss America- Kristine- This book wouldn't have been possible if you wouldn't have loved me so much. Thank you for your love and support. I love you bunches!

It is impossible to thank everyone that has influenced my life. I have been blessed to have people in my life that cared and offered their wisdom to me. I learned early on that not everyone is meant to be there forever, sometimes they are just there for a season or two. I am grateful for everyone that has loved me even for just a season!

To connect with the author: visit the Facebook page:

https://www.facebook.com/SpeaktheTruthMissAmerica/

Special Thanks from Kristine Bunch

Jennifer Pope Baker

Jennifer Pope Baker, Executive Director of Women's Fund of Central Indiana since 1998, has dedicated her career to creating sustainable change for women and girls.

Jennifer became my friend while I was in prison. There she would bring tour groups and I would tell them about the prison programs that enabled women to stay connected with their children. Our friendship built over the span of my incarceration and continued upon my release. Jennifer has continued to encourage me, offer advice and assist me with reintegration. I am blessed to have her as a role model.

Tracey Tabor Williams, DMD

A well-respected dentist in Indianapolis, Indiana, Tracey Williams, DMD, provides preventative, restorative, and cosmetic dental services for adults and children. Dr. Tracey Williams opened her private practice in downtown Indianapolis in 2005. From 2009 to 2015, she has earned recognition as one of the top dentists in metropolitan Indianapolis by a vote of her peers. Additionally, Indianapolis Monthly featured Dr. Williams as a recipient of this honor.

Special thanks to Dr. Tracey Tabor Williams and her incredible staff...

Dr. Williams has taken care of my dental problems since my release. I never imagined that there would be people with such generous hearts.

Hilary Bowe Ricks

Hilary became my attorney at the beginning of my battle. She was the first attorney to believe my truth and offer to help me. I still get emotional each time that I think about it. When the Center on Wrongful Convictions took over my case, Hilary stayed on as pro bono counsel to assist. To this day, she remains my dear friend and a source of inspiration. I wish more people had her willingness to look at a case, see the truth and fight to make that truth known. Our justice system would be very different if we did.

Betsy Marks

I met Betsy Marks through prison ministry. She was a dedicated volunteer. Betsy heard my story and believed in me. She was instrumental in bringing my case to the Center on Wrongful Convictions and creating a group of prayer warriors for me. She remains my friend and is a Board member for my organization JustIS 4 JustUS.

Patricia Messina

Pat works at Northwestern University. Upon my release, Pat assisted me with my resume, interview questions and building confidence. I acquired a wonderful position at Northwestern University thanks to her skills and encouragement. I am blessed to have her as my friend.

Of course, the list of names could continue for pages. I won't do that. I will simply say that everyone that has assisted on this journey has shaped me into the woman I am. I know that each and every one of you helped me to survive and thrive. You all will forever remain in my heart.

I have acknowledged just a few of the people that stepped up to help me re-enter society. There are simply too many to name. I am so grateful for every person that assisted me. I am and will remain in your debt.

This outpouring of love was the inspiration for JustIS 4 JustUS. Another exoneree, Juan Rivera, and myself started this non-for-profit organization to build a community of supporters for exonerees. I believe that we can make a difference for each individual as they are released.

Please consider supporting the innocent. Check out JustIS 4 JustUS.org or check with your local Innocence Projects and make a difference for someone that has no voice.

Much appreciation and love,

~Kristine Bunch

How You Can Help

There are many ways that you can help even without supporting financially. Our goal is to help as many that are in need. The following ways are just a few examples:

Reach out to your state's Innocent Projects. Ask them if they need any assistance, or give financially if possible.

Become a pen pal. Many have lost everything due to their wrongful conviction. A letter or card of support can help them survive another day. They are lost in a dark tunnel and your support could help them see the light at the end of the tunnel.

Offer your services. Exonerees often feel overwhelmed when first released and even riding public transportation can be scary. See if anyone needs a ride to a doctor's visit, or simply a dinner out with a friendly person. It is often lonelier out here then inside walls of a prison.

• Start your own outreach. You can do this independently or with your church. Hold events that raise awareness for exonerees.

Even if you only can support one person, it is making a difference.

That could be the difference that saves one more life from more

despair that freedom presents.

ABOUT THE AUTHOR

Donna Waters lives in Indiana where her days are filled with love and cleaning. As a mother of three, her days are spent managing the household without losing her sanity. She is married to the love of her life who has made her see the bigger picture of life. In her spare time, she enjoys hanging out with her best friend- possibly the only reason she has any sanity left.

Made in the USA
Las Vegas, NV
16 June 2021